THE
CUBAN MISSILE
CRISIS

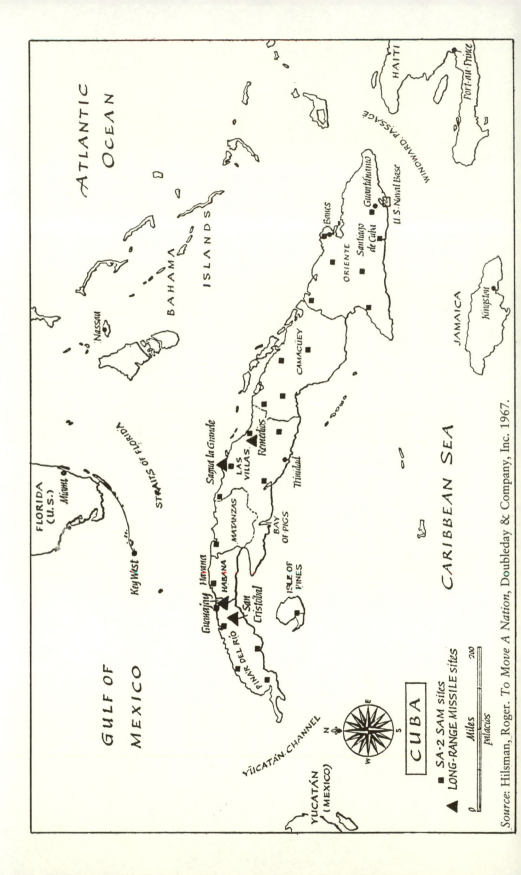

Source: Hilsman, Roger. *To Move A Nation,* Doubleday & Company, Inc. 1967.

THE
CUBAN MISSILE
CRISIS

The Struggle Over Policy

Roger Hilsman

PRAEGER

Westport, Connecticut
London

Library of Congress Cataloging-in-Publication Data

Hilsman, Roger.
    The Cuban missile crisis : the struggle over policy / Roger
Hilsman.
      p.   cm.
    Includes bibliographical references and index.
    ISBN 0–275–95435–8 (alk. paper)
    1. Cuban Missile Crisis, 1962.   I. Title.
E841.H55   1996
973.922—dc20   95–40285

British Library Cataloguing in Publication Data is available.

Library of Congress Catalog Card Number: 95–40285
ISBN: 0–275–95435–8

First published in 1996

Praeger Publishers, 88 Post Road West, Westport, CT 06881
An imprint of Greenwood Publishing Group, Inc.

Printed in the United States of America

The paper used in this book complies with the
Permanent Paper Standard issued by the National
Information Standards Organization (Z39.48–1984).

10 9 8 7 6 5 4 3 2

This book is dedicated to the memory of John F. Kennedy and Robert F. Kennedy, without whose leadership the world might well have suffered nuclear war.

Contents

Photographs follow Chapter 5

Preface

During the Cuban missile crisis, I participated in the deliberations of the United States Intelligence Board and in a number of those in the White House. I also had several sessions during the crisis with President Kennedy alone or in a small group. In my *To Move a Nation: The Politics of Foreign Policy in the Administration of John F. Kennedy,* I wrote four chapters on the Cuban missile crisis, and a number of other authors have also written on the crisis. However, in the last few years new information has become available in bits and pieces that adds considerably to our understanding of what was happening on the Soviet side. In addition, since over 30 years have passed, I am now free to include some material on what was happening on the American side that I was not at liberty to write about before.

Some books have attempted to cover all aspects of the crisis— troop movements, details of the blockade, and all the rest. This book concentrates on the way that President Kennedy, his advisers, and the top officials in the State Department, the Pentagon, and the CIA went about making the decisions about how to deal with the problem of the missiles. It examines in detail the way the participants twisted and turned the evidence trying to understand what the Soviets thought they would accomplish by putting the missiles in Cuba. It also scrutinizes the debate among the top American officials as they tried to find a way for the United States to deal with the problem the missiles posed.

The book also looks at the very human failings shown during the crisis—failings of understanding, failings of human stamina under pressure and lack of sleep, and failings of human relations under extreme stress.

My hope was to try to identify and spell out some lessons that the United States might find useful in dealing with international crises in the years that lie ahead. The result, however, was to discover what seemed to be lessons not just for the United States but for all of humankind.

Roger Hilsman

Acknowledgments

As on so many projects, I am grateful to Eleanor H. Hilsman for her encouragement and support, especially, but also for the endless hours she spent searching libraries for elusive facts and references.

I am also grateful to Charles E. Lindblom, Robert A. Dahl, Vladimir Shamberg, and Alan Platt for their sensitive reading of a very large manuscript on the history of nuclear military strategy and their persuasive advice that I should turn the chapters on the Cuban missile crisis into a separate book.

THE
CUBAN MISSILE
CRISIS

Chapter 1

The Soviet Decision

The Soviets exploded their first atomic weapon in August, 1949. Led by Paul Nitze, head of the Policy Planning Staff at the State Department, part of the American government argued that the United States should immediately rebuild its military forces all across the board. Others thought it would be sufficient to begin to develop both the "super," the hydrogen or H-bomb, and small, tactical, "battlefield" nuclear weapons in large quantities. President Truman was committed to keeping the defense budget under the $15 billion ceiling he had promised in the presidential campaign of 1948, so he sided with those who thought a buildup in nuclear weapons would be enough.

Then came the North Korean attack on South Korea. Everywhere in the West people assumed that the Soviets had ordered the North Koreans to attack. No one at the time had any reason to believe otherwise. Opinion was unanimous that the Soviets, having broken the West's monopoly of atomic bombs, had decided that the time had come to test both the defenses of the West and its will.

Truman promptly gave up trying to keep the defense budget low and agreed to a rearmament program. The defense budget went from $17.7 billion in fiscal year 1950 to $53.4 billion in fiscal year 1951. A decision was made for a troop buildup in Europe, and additional American divisions began to arrive shortly thereafter. The other Allies followed with increases of their own. A decision was also made to rearm Germany. In the most important decision of all the Allies also agreed to form NATO—the North Atlantic Treaty Organization—the first international force with a unified command ever established in the absence of actual war. Dwight D. Eisenhower was given command.

The situation seemed to have been stabilized. Then during the latter part of the Eisenhower administration, the evidence mounted that the Soviets were engaged in a large-scale buildup of intercontinental ballistic missiles armed with nuclear warheads. The CIA estimated that the Soviets would draw decisively ahead of the United States in its missile stockpile in no more than two or three years, that is, by 1962 or 1963.

Air Force estimates of Soviet missile production were even higher. Both the CIA and the Air Force leaked their estimates to sympathetic members of Congress and the press. It was widely believed that if the Soviet Union was not already ahead of the United States in missiles, it soon would be. In the election campaign of 1960, John F. Kennedy and the Democrats made much of this upcoming "missile gap," as it was called, which clearly contributed to their victory.

THE MISSILE GAP[1]

When the Soviets completed their first experiments with rockets and began to lay out their longer-range program, they decided on a bold move. They elected to skip the logical next step—rockets of about 350,000 pounds of thrust like the U.S. Atlas—and to leap to giants of about 800,000 pounds thrust. The result was the behemoth that in 1957 launched the Soviet *Sputnik,* the first man-made earth satellite, and that gave the Soviets the thrust for their many other space achievements, including putting the first man in space, Yuri Gagarin. But this rocket was also intended to serve as the workhorse of the Soviet ICBM force, and American intelligence was rightly impressed.

On August 27, 1957, the United States detected a successful Soviet test firing of an ICBM. Four times that year, the United States tried to fire a Thor intermediate-range missile, and all four attempts failed. In June, 1957, the United States tried to fire an Atlas ICBM, and that, too, failed. The U.S. Navy tried to fire the Vanguard missile, and it also failed.

The Soviets then successfully tested the SS–6, a heavy ICBM. On October 4, 1957, they successfully launched the first man-made satellite—Sputnik. A month later they orbited a live dog—and American intelligence intercepted the television photos of the dog blinking into the camera.

In 1957–1958, British pilots also began flying the U–2 over the Soviet Union.

Both American and British intelligence became convinced that the Soviets were just about ready to go from research ICBM test firings to an actual deployment program. Allied intelligence picked up rumors that the ICBMs were being deployed at Plesetsk near the Arctic Circle, and on May 1, 1960, a U–2, piloted by Gary Powers, was dispatched to investigate. It was shot down, there was a worldwide political brouhaha, and President Eisenhower was forced to declare that no more U–2s would be flown over the Soviet Union.

His decision was made considerably easier by the fact that a new Soviet antiaircraft SAM had been observed in November of 1957, the SA–2, that seemed to be capable of shooting down a U–2. The SA–2s were now being deployed, and the U–2 was therefore at the end of its usefulness in flying over the Soviet Union. Another consideration was that a successor was very close to becoming operational—the SR–71, Blackbird, which could fly at an altitude of 85,000 feet and at a speed three times that of sound. Still another consideration was the development of a picture-taking satellite, code-named Corona. It became operational in 1959, but the first 12 flights were plagued by repeated failures—once the rocket exploded on the launching pad, three times the satellite failed to reach its orbit, twice the satellite went into an unusable orbit, once the film pod ejected prematurely, and three times the camera failed. Still at the time of Eisenhower's pledge on the U–2, it seemed likely that the Corona's problems would be solved in due time.

Getting pictures of the Plesetsk area was extremely difficult because of the almost constant cloud cover in the northern areas of the Soviet Union. In fact, the reason that Eisenhower had been persuaded to authorize the May 1 flight just when he was about to meet with Khrushchev, was that May 1 was the only day for many weeks for which clear weather had been predicted over Plesetsk.

Army intelligence in this period began to estimate that the Soviets would soon have about 200 ICBMs deployed. The Air Force thought it would be more like 700.

In any case, as the intelligence community as a whole looked at their estimates in 1958, 1959, and 1960 and even through the first half of 1961, they saw a missile gap developing that would come to a peak about 1963 or 1964.

The idea has since taken root that the so-called missile gap meant that in 1960 the Soviet Union was *already* ahead of the United States in deployed ICBMs. In fact, President Eisenhower appointed the noted scientist George B. Kistiakowsky to head a panel of experts to study the U–2 photos and all other intelligence available, and this panel concluded that no missile gap existed *at that time.*

But what worried the intelligence community was not a present gap, but a *future* one. The missile gap that worried the intelligence community and that they leaked to their friends in Congress and the press was a *projected* gap. The intelligence community compared the American plans for building ICBMs, which they of course had readily available, to what the community *estimated* were the Soviet plans and foresaw a gap developing in 1963, or at the latest, 1964.

Both the intelligence community and the Air Force made a major effort through orthodox channels to win approval for a crash ICBM program. But the Eisenhower administration argued that the difference would be made up by the American superiority in manned bombers, although it reluctantly granted a small increase in the number of missiles to be produced. However, the intelligence community thought that the increase was much too small to overcome the potential gap.

Inevitably, the more convinced among the Air Force and intelligence people then tried an end run through leaks to members of Congress and newspaper columnists. When Kennedy became president, he ordered another increase in the number of missiles to be produced, but most of the people in the Air Force and intelligence community who were concerned about the problem thought it was not enough to close the upcoming missile gap. President Kennedy and his administration agreed that a gap would develop over the next few years. But they believed the kind of increase that was wanted would be so damaging to the economy that they, too, hoped that the American superiority in manned bombers would make up the difference.

In the meantime, the Soviets continued to deploy their giant rocket as an ICBM near Plesetsk. But this behemoth that both the Soviets and the Americans thought would give the Soviet Union a decisive advantage turned out to be a bitter disappointment. For the Soviets discovered immediately—and the Americans only much later—that this huge missile was just too big and bulky to serve as a practical weapon. The Soviets had to start again from the beginning to design a newer, smaller, more streamlined missile. The Soviet ICBM program must have been set back many months.

The Soviets, of course, knew that their hopes of catching up with the United States had been drastically set back, but so long as the Americans did not know the true situation the Soviets still enjoyed the immediate benefits of seeming to be about to catch up with the United States or conceivably of having just surpassed it.

Certainly at the beginning of the Kennedy administration the Soviets acted as if they were supremely confident of their strength. Shortly before Kennedy's inauguration, Khrushchev had made a belligerent speech announcing support for "wars of national liberation." And later that year at his meeting with Kennedy in Vienna, Khrushchev had blustered that Berlin "belongs to us," and shortly afterward the East Germans began a crash effort to build the Berlin Wall.

When the Kennedy administration took office in 1961, the evidence on the Soviet missile deployment was still inconclusive. Even as late as June, 1961, after Kennedy had been in office for five months, the evidence was contradictory. The June National Intelligence Estimate showed that the intelligence community was badly split. The Air Force was estimating that the Soviets had as many as 300 ICBMs deployed. The Navy was estimating less than a dozen. The CIA and the State Department intelligence people split the difference with an estimate of 150. Secretary McNamara was impatient at the wide difference of opinion and pressed for a greater intelligence effort.

Parenthetically, it should be noted that McNamara claimed in his book, *In Retrospect, the Tragedy and Lessons of Vietnam*, published in 1995, that as soon as he took office he had "spent days . . . personally reviewing hundreds of photographs of Soviet missile sites that had been the basis for the air force report" and came to the conclusion that there was no missile gap, that the United States was ahead.[2] He said as much in a press conference and caused a storm of outrage on Capitol Hill. In fact, McNamara's conclusion was only a hunch, with no hard evidence to back it up, and in matters as serious as this, hunches should not be the basis for policy decisions. He offered Kennedy his resignation, but Kennedy told him to forget it, that we all put our foot in our mouth once in a while and that the storm would blow over.

Probably as a consequence of this incident, what McNamara said to the intelligence community at the time was only that he found defense planning difficult when there were such wide gaps between the Air Force estimate, the Navy estimate, and the joint CIA-State Department estimate.

Then during the summer of 1961, the United States flew its first successful Corona satellites and discovered the true situation. Rather than a missile gap in favor of the Soviet Union there was one in favor of the United States.

The first big success of the Corona was the 14th mission, which took pictures of the Soviet bomber base at Mys Shmidta in the Russian Far East, only 400 miles from Nome, Alaska. This was followed by 5 more successful missions, and the intelligence community in September, 1961, was able with complete confidence to revise its estimate down from 140 to 200 Soviet ICBM launchers to a figure of 10 to 25.

Jumping ahead for a moment, during the Cuban missile crisis, the United States had 140 ICBMs on alert ready to fire at the Soviet homeland. For the Soviet Union, the generally accepted figure derived from satellite reconnaissance is 44 ICBMs on alert and ready to fire on the American homeland. One of the Soviet participants in a postmortem conference of Soviets, Cubans, and Americans in Moscow in 1989 claimed that he had examined the Soviet archives and had concluded that the number was only 20. The reluctance to accept this figure is based not only on hard satellite intelligence but also on the fact that the Soviet participants were pushing what might be termed a revisionist view on several other points as well.

In addition to ICBMs, the United States also had on continuous airborne alert during the crisis about 200 manned bombers capable of dropping nuclear bombs on the Soviet homeland. The Soviets also had a much smaller number of manned bombers capable of dropping nuclear bombs on the American homeland, although for most of the Soviet bombers it would have to be a one-way flight.

In any case, it was only long after the crisis was over that the United States learned the reason that the predicted missile gap had not materialized. The huge rocket that had orbited Yuri Gagarin had turned out to be just too big and too bulky to serve as an operational ICBM.

SHOULD THE SOVIETS BE TOLD?

For several weeks the top levels of the Kennedy administration and the intelligence community agonized over whether or not to tell the Soviets what it now knew. Everyone understood that a deliberate decision to tell the Soviets entailed significant risks. Forewarned, the Soviets would undoubtedly speed up their ICBM program. They would do so anyway, of course, but letting them know that the United States knew the true situation meant the speedup would be sooner rather than later and larger rather than smaller.

On the other hand, Khrushchev's several ultimata on Berlin indicated that if he were allowed to continue to assume that the United States still believed in the missile gap, he would very probably bring the world dangerously close to war. On balance, it seemed wiser to go ahead and tell the Soviets that the United States now knew the truth, in spite of misgivings in the intelligence community that revealing the information might give the Soviets clues about the American intelligence techniques. And President Kennedy came to agree with those who argued for disclosure.

The means used to tell the Soviets that the United States now knew were carefully crafted. Both public and subterranean channels were used.

If public disclosure was made by the president, the secretary of state, or the secretary of defense, it might appear threatening. On the other hand, the person chosen had to be high enough in rank to be credible. So the decision was to have the public announcement made by Roswell Gilpatric, the *deputy* secretary of defense, and he did so in a dry, numbers-laden, unprovocative speech given in October, 1961.

The subterranean channel chosen was a round of briefings of the

NATO Allies—with pictures. The briefings deliberately included some Allies who the United States knew were penetrated by KGB agents. In this way the message carried openly by the Gilpatric speech would be reinforced and confirmed through Soviet intelligence channels, which the Soviet leadership would probably find more persuasive than a mere speech.

SOVIET MOTIVATIONS

When the U.S. government decided to tell the Soviets that it had learned that the missile gap favored the United States, it fully understood that the Soviets would feel impelled to do something drastic to right the balance. What the United States expected the Soviets to do was embark upon a crash ICBM program. Instead they opted for putting MRBMs and IRBMs in Cuba. Why?

Consider the view from Moscow when President Kennedy took office in January of 1961, 18 months before the missile decision. In the Soviet Union, the domestic situation was good. Work was proceeding on the party program and on the 20-year plan for increasing domestic production.

The world situation was also good. First and foremost, the Soviets were still basking in the afterglow of the Sputnik success, and the world generally assumed that the military and strategic balance had significantly shifted in the Soviets' favor.

In the United States, a new, young, and presumably inexperienced president had just taken over the reins of government after an extremely close election, and he seemed to have few prospects except continued deadlock politically and recession economically. The Atlantic community had made little progress toward unity. The underdeveloped world was in ferment, offering the Soviet Union exciting prospects. Africa, Latin America, and Southeast Asia all seemed full of opportunities. Finally, although the Sino-Soviet dispute continued to be extremely disturbing, there was still hope that it could be contained. In spite of the fact that the dispute had continued during the recent meeting of the 81 Communist parties, a *modus vivendi* with the Chinese still seemed possible.

Khrushchev expressed his satisfaction with all these favorable prospects in his speech of January 6, 1961, just before Kennedy took office. Confidently, he laid out an ambitious and aggressive program to extend Communist influence throughout the world—from Berlin, where he revived threats of an ultimatum, to the underdeveloped world, which he invited to embark on new and better "wars of national liberation."

But by the spring of 1962, things looked quite different to Moscow. President Kennedy and the West had stood firm on Berlin. There had been movement in the Atlantic community toward unity. The difficulties of dealing with the underdeveloped world were becoming clearer to the Soviet leadership—the expense of foreign aid, the political instability of the emerging nations, their touchiness, their extremist nationalisms, their inexperience, and also their instinct and skill in playing the great powers off against each other rather than being dominated by one of them.

And the Sino-Soviet dispute had gotten out of hand. In one sense Communism is a doctrine for acquiring and using power, and the trouble was that the Chinese were behaving like Communists. The dispute had come to have a dynamism of its own.

Domestically, the Soviet leaders found that the demands they had themselves set in motion with "de-Stalinization" and promises of consumers' goods had become a tiger they were finding difficult to ride. There were just not enough resources to meet the whole long list of demands—a better life for consumers; the needs of the space program, prestigious though it might be; the foreign aid required to play an active, worldwide role; and, above all, the costs of achieving military supremacy.

The bold leap to the huge rockets of 800,000-pound thrust failed, as we saw. So now in addition to all the other demands on scarce resources, the Soviet leadership was faced with a missile gap in favor of the United States. The only consolation was that the United States had not yet learned the true situation and still believed that the missile gap favored the Soviet Union.

So for the Soviet leadership the signals from Gilpatric's speech and the reports of their agents of the briefings given the NATO countries were horrendous. It was not so much the fact that the Americans had military superiority—the Soviets knew that already. What was bound to alarm them much more was that the Americans now *knew* that they had military superiority.

The Soviets quickly realized that to have reached this conclusion that the missile gap was in their favor, the Americans must have made an intelligence breakthrough. It was obvious to the Soviets that the Americans could not have calculated the total numbers of deployed Soviet missiles unless they had found a way to pinpoint where those missiles were actually located.

A relatively "soft" ICBM system with somewhat cumbersome launching techniques, which is what the Soviets had at that time, is an effective weapon for both a first strike and a second, retaliatory strike so long as the locations of the launching pads are secret. However, if the enemy has a map with all the pads plotted, the system will retain some of its utility as a first-strike weapon, but almost none as a second-strike weapon. The whole Soviet ICBM system was suddenly obsolescent.

Not only had the military balance turned decisively against the Soviets but so had the political balance. When the United States thought it was behind in the missile race, the Soviets did not hesitate to turn the screws on Berlin even though they knew the truth. It was simply inconceivable to the Soviets that the United States would not use their newfound advantage in a similar way, to accomplish substantial political gains.

While the Soviet leaders fretted over these intractable problems Castro clamored more and more insistently for military protection, couching his pleas so as to magnify the threat of an American invasion.

A NEW BAY OF PIGS?

Khrushchev says in his memoirs that the idea of putting missiles in Cuba was his own. It came to him during a visit to Bulgaria while he was pacing up and down alone in his hotel room worrying about the fact that the Americans were not only ahead in ICBMs but knew that they were ahead.

Khrushchev claims that his principal worry was not really the missile gap in reverse but that the United States might launch another Bay of Pigs invasion.[3] But Khrushchev knew that President Kennedy had been pressed hard by both the CIA and the Joint Chiefs of Staff to intervene with American forces when the Bay of Pigs invasion began to fail and that Kennedy had adamantly refused. Khrushchev also knew all about the criticism that Kennedy took for this refusal and that in spite of the criticism Kennedy had not ordered any military preparations whatsoever for an invasion of Cuba.

Even though Castro undoubtedly knew that Kennedy had refused the CIA and Pentagon pleas to permit the use of American troops at the time of the Bay of Pigs, it is conceivable that Castro might still have feared an invasion, since his independent intelligence resources were probably limited to agents within the Cuban communities in New York and Florida. But Khrushchev did not lack for intelligence.

If anyone has any doubts that Khrushchev's claim that he feared a American invasion of Cuba was propaganda for his foreign audience and rationalization for his domestic one, it is constructive to consider the similar situation the United States faced in Asia in 1962—what the Chinese called the Year of the Tiger. Chiang Kai-shek, head of the Nationalist regime in Taiwan, wanted the United States to back him in an invasion of the mainland to block and preempt the invasion of Taiwan he claimed was being prepared by the Communists. The CIA station chief in Taiwan was Ray Cline, who was a close friend of Chiang's son, Chiang Ching-Kuo, the head of Taiwan's CIA. Cline made a special trip to the United States to present the case for an invasion to President Kennedy and the NSC.

After Cline was finished talking, McNamara in a brilliant demonstration of his skill with numbers, rebutted. Pointing out that a seaborne assault on a hostile shore, as the landings at Anzio and Normandy demonstrated, is the most difficult of all military operations, he proceeded to outline the forces that would be necessary— the number of troops, artillery, tanks, and other equipment that the invading force would need. Then he totaled up the vast number of ships, landing craft, and warplanes for air cover. And then he described the U–2 and other reconnaissance that had been conducted over the previous weeks, and said flatly that none of these many missions had revealed anything that even remotely resembled an invasion force. With his tail between his legs, Cline went back to Taiwan, and a few weeks later Chiang Ching-kuo conceded that the Year of the Tiger was over.

In the case of the Cuban missile crisis, Khrushchev had better intelligence available to him than the United States had had at the time of the Year of the Tiger, and there is simply no doubt that Khrushchev knew that the United States had made no preparations whatsoever for an invasion of Cuba.[4]

It should also be noted that in a conference in Moscow in January, 1989, with Soviet, American, and Cuban participants, to discuss the

Cuban missile crisis, the Cuban representatives "sharply contra-dicted" Khrushchev's claim that the missiles were needed to defend Cuba against an invasion, dismissing the utility of Soviet nuclear missiles in Cuba for either deterrence or defense. They said that Castro had accepted the Soviet missiles for two reasons: (1) the missiles would shift the global correlation of forces in favor of socialism and (2) Cuba should accept "its share of the risk" since the Soviets had already taken some risks in support of the Cuban revolution. It should also be noted that Castro himself made a similar statement in an interview with *Le Monde* March 22 and 23, 1963.

So Khrushchev's claim that the motive for putting the missiles in Cuba was fear of another Bay of Pigs can be dismissed as both rationalization and propaganda.

OPERATION MONGOOSE

Another charge is that what was agitating both Castro and Khru-shchev was not the threat of an actual invasion by American troops but a CIA attempt to overthrow Castro by covert means. After the Bay of Pigs fiasco, a CIA operation was set up under the code name *Mongoose,* headed by Edward Lansdale, the CIA officer who was given much credit for helping Magsaysay put down the Communist Hukbalahaps in the Philippines and for running the CIA covert operations in Vietnam at the time of Dienbienphu.

Thirty years later in a CIA-sponsored conference on the Cuban missile crisis, a CIA official involved with Mongoose said that the idea of a covert operation to "destabilize" Castro and his government came from the Kennedy White House, and that the CIA was considerably less than enthusiastic about the idea. By 1962, Lansdale was very unpopular indeed within the CIA, and this might also have had something to do with the CIA's lack of enthusiasm.

But it is also true that Mongoose was not only ineffective, but actually a little silly. One idea the Mongoose team developed was to plant some shampoo in the supplies used by Castro's barber that would make Castro's beard fall out—an idea that was never implemented.

Another, equally silly idea *was* implemented, but it is doubtful that Castro learned about it until many years later. The Mongoose team succeeded in contaminating a shipload of sugar bound from Cuba to the Soviet Union with a chemical that would cause nausea and vomiting—the idea being to spread distrust of Cuban sugar in the Soviet population. When Kennedy heard about the operation, he ordered Lansdale to buy the whole shipload of sugar and dump it at sea—which was done.

President Kennedy was well aware both of the inadequacies of "covert operations" and of the firm hold that Castro had on Cuba, and it is very doubtful that he thought that Mongoose's "destabilizing" efforts would really affect Castro's position. The Kennedy White House did urge the CIA to set up Mongoose and to put Lansdale in charge. But rather than any hope that covert action would have any real success, the motive was more likely to permit the Kennedy White House to say to its domestic political opponents who were calling for "action" to deal with Castro and Cuba that something was indeed being done.

In any case, Operation Mongoose in its totality was nothing more than a pinprick. It mounted no notable operations, and it is doubtful if Castro was even aware of most of the operations it did try to mount.

The truth of the matter is that there were no conceivable circumstances in which the Soviet Union would have taken even the tiniest risk of war with the United States to save Castro and a Communist Cuba. What was really agitating Khrushchev as he paced up and down his hotel room in Bulgaria and what loomed so ominously over everything else was, as Khrushchev wrote in his memoirs, "what the West likes to call the 'balance of power.' "

In a memo written in the few days after the missiles were discovered, the Sovietologists in the State Department's Bureau of Intelligence and Research (INR), of which I was the director, concluded that the Soviet leadership had apparently hit upon the idea of putting the MRBMs and IRBMs in Cuba as a generalized, strategic response to this whole set of problems that faced them—military, economic, and political.[5]

The Soviet leadership probably understood that sending missiles to Cuba was not much more than a temporary, expedient, and essentially stopgap solution to their problems. But they had a vast oversupply of the older 1,000-mile MRBMs (SS–4s) and 2,000-mile IRBMs (SS–5s). So sending them to Cuba would give the Soviets a cheap and immediate substitute for the newer, more expensive ICBMs and let them stretch out the ICBM program to ease the pressure on resources.[6]

At the same time, sending MRBMs and IRBMs to Cuba would meet Castro's demands and protect what had become, since Castro's self-proclaimed membership in the Communist bloc, not just another third-world ally as a result of a "war of national liberation" but the first opportunity to project Soviet power into the Western Hemisphere.

Thus the motive for the decision was strategic in the broad sense that a general improvement in the Soviet military position would affect the entire political context, strengthening the Soviet Union's hand for dealing with the whole range of problems facing it and unanticipated problems as well.

But even though general rather than specific security and foreign policy goals were the principal motive of the Soviet decision to deploy missiles to Cuba, once the deployment was accomplished, it promised enticing prospects for specific gains in foreign policy and ancillary benefits that would appeal to various segments of the Soviet leadership.

A substantial missile force in Cuba would strengthen the over-all Soviet position, and Soviet leverage on Berlin would be significantly improved. NATO would surely be shaken and the chances of the United States successfully creating a NATO multilateral force, which was being discussed at the time, would be greatly reduced.

In Latin America other potential "Castros" would be encouraged. American power would be less impressive and American protection less desirable, and some of the Latin American states would move in the Soviet direction even if their governments were not overthrown.

In Asia, a successful move in Cuba would cut the ground from under the Chinese Communists and go far toward convincing Communists everywhere that Soviet leadership was strong and that Soviet methods in dealing with the "imperialists" were effective.

THE SOVIET PLAN

As we now know, the Soviet plan was in two phases. In the first phase, Cuba was to be ringed with defenses—24 batteries of surface-to-air antiaircraft missiles with a slant range of 25 miles, over 100 MIG fighter planes, short-range harbor defense missiles (with a range of 35 to 40 miles), coastal patrol boats armed with ship-to-ship missiles, and IL–28 light bombers.

The second phase was to deploy to Cuba six battalions of the MRBMs and four battalions of the IRBMs. In western Cuba, three battalions of the MRBMs were to be at San Cristóbal and three at Sagua la Grande. In central Cuba two battalions of the IRBMs were to be at Guanajay and two more battalions at Remedios. Thus San Cristóbal and Sagua la Grande would each have 12 launching pads and Guanajay and Remedios would each have eight—for a total of forty pads. Each pad was to be equipped with 2 missiles, so 40 missiles could be fired in an initial salvo and 40 more could be launched in a follow-on.

The warheads for the MRBMs and IRBMs had the explosive force of 1 megaton, that is, the equivalent of 1 *million* tons of TNT. By comparison, the bomb that destroyed Hiroshima had an explosive force of 14 kilotons, that is, fourteen *thousand* pounds of TNT.

During the crisis, over 20 cruise missile installations were also identified. Such missiles normally carry nuclear warheads and have a range of several hundred miles, but it is not clear just what their targets were to be. However, the most likely possibility would have been troop concentrations in Florida if the United States started preparing for an invasion.

It was to be a major military deployment, in some ways as complicated to plan and carry out as a landing on a hostile shore, such as the Normandy, Anzio, and Inchon landings. Each of the 24 antiaircraft sites was to have 24 missiles thirty feet long—a total of 576 missiles—and a variety of special trailers, fueling trucks, and radar vans. The MRBM and IRBM missile battalions were to have a total of 80 missiles, as already mentioned, and dozens of special vehicles, missile erectors, and personnel carriers.[7]

The missile forces would be accompanied by four battle groups of special ground troops, a total of about 42,000 men. These troops were to be armed with tactical nuclear weapons with a range of 40 kilometers to protect the missiles from ground attack, either by invasion or from the American base at Guantánamo. These ground elements were a formidable force of infantry, artillery, and battlefield nuclear weapons. It is probably no accident that if Castro had ever taken a notion to try to take over the missiles for himself, this force could have defeated the whole Cuban army in very short order.[8]

The grand total of men, weapons, vehicles, and materiel was staggering. A measure of its magnitude is the fact that a ship can carry 20 to 30 railroad trainloads of materiel and that the deployment required more than 100 ships to carry it all—making a total of 2,000 to 3,000 trainloads of war materiel.

Planning and coordinating a military movement of this magnitude and rescheduling and assembling the necessary shipping probably took several weeks. Since the first of the shipments began to arrive in Cuban ports near the end of July, the latest the decision could have been made was probably early in June.

The other evidence available also points to June. Throughout the spring of 1962, Castro apparently pressed for commitments the Soviets were reluctant to give. In March, April, and May the strains in Cuban-Soviet relations were severe, highlighted by Castro's Escalente purges, which eliminated some of the more militant old-time Communists from his government. Then, toward the end of June, the tension seemed to ease. Castro made a strange speech to some departing Soviet technicians, apologizing for the "poor treatment" they had received. Early in July Castro sent his brother, Raúl, on a flying visit to Moscow and following his return, Castro made a speech saying that the country was threatened by neither internal uprisings nor exile landings, but only by an American invasion—which, he said, "we can now repel."

NOTES

1. What follows is based on the chapters dealing with the Cuban missile crisis in my *To Move a Nation: The Politics of Foreign Policy in the Administration of John F. Kennedy* (Garden City, NY: Doubleday, 1967), and my *The Politics of Policy Making in Defense and Foreign Affairs: Conceptual Models and Bureaucratic Politics,* 3rd ed. (Englewood Cliffs, NJ: Prentice Hall, 1993). But it has been revised and expanded to take advantage of the wealth of new material that has recently become available.

2. With Brian VanDeMark (New York: Times Books), pp. 20–21.

3. Strobe Talbot, translator and editor, *Khrushchev Remembers* (Boston: Little, Brown, 1970), pp. 491–95.

4. Some of the American analysts who have written about their participation in the joint Soviet, Cuban, and American postmortems of the crisis many years later treat the attempts by the Soviet participants to support Khrushchev's claims that he feared an invasion seriously. It is obvious that if they subjected the Soviet claims to critical scrutiny it would probably have jeopardized their participation in any future conferences as well as any possibility of some day gaining access to Soviet archives. On the other hand, their willingness to accept some of the other Soviet claims cannot be so easily explained. On these points they seem to have been both naive and gullible.

5. See my *To Move a Nation,* Chapter 13. It might be added that the analysis made by the INR sovietologists, principally Helmut Sonnenfeldt and Joseph W. Neubert, has been supported by the evidence that has become available since the analysis was written, including Khrushchev's memoirs, which are very pertinent even though they are obviously both biased and incomplete.

6. The fact that the Soviets had so massively overproduced MRBMs and IRBMs has been a puzzle to Western analysts. The most persuasive explanation is that in the Soviet Union the artillery was given responsibility for missiles rather than the Air Force, as in the United States.

Air Forces generally follow a "standard operating procedure" (SOP) of providing a finite number of planes with which to fight a war. At the beginning of World War II, for example, President Roosevelt startled both our Allies and Hitler by announcing that the United States had set itself the goal of producing 45,000 aircraft in 1942 and 100,000 in 1943. In producing artillery guns and shells, however, most countries follow an SOP of providing a production capacity that will give them so many guns and so many millions of rounds of ammunition *per month of fighting,* rather than a finite number for the whole war.

Organizational SOP also seems to account for the puzzling failure of the Soviet missile construction battalions to camouflage their work from the very beginning, rather than waiting until the sites were almost completed. The construction battalions were following the SOP for constructing sites in the Soviet Union, apparently without anyone thinking how different the situation in Cuba was—i.e., without anyone thinking that camouflage was needed for the missile sites in Cuba from the very beginning.

7. What is referred to here as an MRBM was designated by American intelligence as the SS–4, a single-stage rocket. Without the nose cone, which is how it was normally transported, it was 59 feet long. What is referred to here as an IRBM was designated by American intelligence as the SS–5, also a single-stage rocket. Without its nose cone it was 82 feet long, as well as being 8 feet in diameter.

8. As described in Chapter 8, the United States believed at the time the Soviet ground forces numbered only about 20,000 men and did not learn that the true total was about 42,000 until long after the crisis had been resolved. But low-level reconnaissance flights instituted just after the crisis became public on October 23 over the next two or three days identified 14 of the battlefield nuclear missile launchers, the weapon that the Soviets called the *Luna* and American intelligence called the *Frog*.

Chapter 2

The Intelligence Story

The United States learned that arms were being shipped to Cuba as soon as the first of them began to arrive in late July, 1962. But it was not until October 14 that American intelligence learned that the shipments included long-range nuclear missiles.

The Soviets cloaked the movement of both the defensive and the offensive arms with great secrecy. Very few ports were used. Cubans living near the docks were evacuated. High fences were put up and guarded by Soviet soldiers. Soviet personnel also did most of the unloading. The equipment was landed at night, readied for transport by road, and moved out in night convoys to make room for the next shipment. Sites had been readied in remote areas, naturally screened by hills and woods, and the population in the areas had been evacuated.

Once the equipment reached these sites, speed was added to security—no attempt was made to camouflage until after a weapon was operational. And the measures taken to ensure speed were extraordinary. Even the concrete arches in the buildings intended to be used as nuclear storage magazines were prefabricated—cast in the Soviet Union and shipped the whole fantastic distance to Cuba.

Initially no public announcement was made, even of the agreement to supply Cuba with conventional arms. Then in late August, after the shipments had been going on for a month and the first newspaper stories about the arms shipments had come out of Washington, "Che" Guevara visited Moscow, and this occasion was used to acknowledge the arms shipments. A joint communiqué issued on September 22 stated that the Soviet Union had agreed to help Cuba meet threats from "aggressive imperialist quarters" by delivering "armaments and sending technical specialists for training Cuban servicemen."

"COVER AND DECEPTION"

Thereafter, the Soviets' public and diplomatic stance was what strategic planners would call a program for "cover and deception." In early September the Soviet ambassador to the United States, Anatoly Dobrynin, on separate occasions told both Robert Kennedy and Theodore Sorensen, the president's special assistant, that the equipment they were sending to Cuba was "defensive in nature and did not represent any threat to the security of the United States." On September 11, 1962, in a public, official statement, the Soviets said that there was

> no need for the Soviet Union to shift its weapons for the repulsion of aggression, for a retaliatory blow, to any other country, for instance Cuba. Our nuclear weapons are so powerful in their explosive force and the Soviet Union has so powerful rockets to carry these nuclear warheads, that there is no need to search for sites for them beyond the boundaries of the Soviet Union.

Another instrument of deception was Georgi Bolshakov, a public information officer in the Soviet embassy in Washington, who had arranged for Aleksei Adzhubei, Khrushchev's son-in-law, to interview President Kennedy. In Moscow in early October, Khrushchev told Bolshakov to tell the Americans that the arms the Soviets were sending to Cuba were "intended" only for defensive purposes. Mikoyan, deputy premier of the Soviet union, was also present in Khrushchev's meeting with Bolshakov; and he went further still, making a special point that President Kennedy himself should be made to understand that the Soviets were sending only antiaircraft missiles to Cuba, which could not reach American targets. Bolshakov took the conversation down in his notebook to be sure he had it straight, and diligently passed the word when he got back to Washington.

On October 13, Chester Bowles, the undersecretary of state, had a long conversation with Soviet Ambassador Dobrynin and pressed him very hard on the question of whether the Soviets intended to put "offensive weapons" in Cuba. The ambassador convincingly and repeatedly denied any such intention.

In Moscow a few days later, on October 16, Khrushchev repeated to the American ambassador, Foy D. Kohler, his denials that any offensive weapons were being sent to Cuba.

On September 25, Castro announced an agreement with the Soviet Union to construct a fishing port in Cuba, and this raised a storm of public suspicion in the United States that what was really being built was a submarine or naval base. Khrushchev was vacationing in the Crimea at the time, but shortly after he returned—on October 16—he told Ambassador Kohler that he was furious at Castro for this premature announcement; that it would not have occurred if he had not been away; and that the last thing in the world that he, Khrushchev, wanted to do was to embarrass President Kennedy on the eve of congressional elections. Soviet "purposes" in Cuba, Khrushchev said, were wholly defensive.

Even as late as October 18, the Soviet foreign minister, Andrei Gromyko, personally assured President Kennedy on a visit to Washington that Soviet aid to Cuba "pursued solely the purpose of contributing to the defense capabilities of Cuba," that "training by Soviet specialists of Cuban nationals in handling defensive armaments was by no means offensive," and that "if it were otherwise, the Soviet government would never become involved in such assistance."

Hearing this, Kennedy resisted the temptation to show Gromyko the U–2 photos, which he had in the drawer of his desk, but sent for and read aloud to Gromyko the public statements that he, Kennedy, had made in September warning the Soviets against putting missiles into Cuba.

Going over the record of this conversation the next day and comparing it with the earlier conversations, analysts in the State Department's Bureau of Intelligence and Research, of which I was the director, noticed something peculiar. On September 30, Navy planes watching Soviet ships at sea on their way to Cuba had taken pictures of some crates on the deck of one of the ships, crates of a peculiar size and shape that were similar to those the Soviets had used to ship IL–28 light bombers to Egypt and Indonesia. Unaccountably, the pictures had come to Washington through roundabout channels rather than direct and were not distributed until October 9. The reason that Bowles had pressed Dobrynin so hard on "offensive weapons" was that he had just seen the pictures of these crates and had uppermost in his mind the strong possibility that they contained IL–28 light bombers.

What struck us in the Bureau of Intelligence and Research as peculiar was that although Dobrynin seemed to have had no knowledge of the decision to put missiles in Cuba, the people reading his cables in Moscow certainly did. Dobrynin would have reported his conversations with Bowles in full detail, and Moscow would most likely have interpreted Bowles' comments as referring to missiles. Thus when Khrushchev had his conversation with Kohler on October 16, seven days later, he must have assumed that the United States knew about the missiles—or at least Moscow must have considered that it was a very real possibility that the United States knew about the missiles. And certainly if Moscow had any remaining doubts that the United States knew, they would have been dispelled when the president had his conversation with Gromyko and read aloud his September warnings, which so specifically and pointedly referred to missiles.

Before the president made any decisions about how to handle the crisis, it was vital for him to know that the Soviets probably thought the U.S. government already knew about the missiles when Khrushchev talked to Kohler and Gromyko had his conversation with the president. So I immediately passed our conclusions along to the White House.

But all this came later. The Soviets did, in fact, draw a veil of secrecy and deception around their buildup of arms in Cuba—being just as secretive about conventional arms as about the missiles.

THE SOURCES OF INTELLIGENCE

To pierce this veil of secrecy and deception, the United States had to rely on four major sources of intelligence. One was routine shipping intelligence. As a matter of course, the United States knew what ships went to Cuba, whether from Communist or "free-world" ports. Second, there was a steady flow of reports from refugees. Third, there were the reports of actual intelligence agents inside Cuba. And, finally, there were the photographs supplied by the U–2 overflights.[1]

Shipping intelligence did not reveal the contents of the ships. Refugee reports attempted to guess what was under the canvas on the trailers the refugees saw, but the reports varied widely in reliability about what the refugees had actually seen, and even more in what they imagined—ranging from sober and accurate observations to the wildest kind of rumor. Refugee reports also trailed events by days or even weeks, depending on how long it took a particular refugee to get out of Cuba to a place where he or she could be questioned.

Another problem with refugee reports was simply one of mass. As the true colors of the Castro regime began to show, the hundreds of refugees became thousands. The CIA increased the staff of its interrogation center at Opa-Locka, Florida, and of its research offices in Washington devoted to collating, comparing, and studying the interrogation results. But the stream of refugees continued and processing frequently fell behind.

The United States Intelligence Board (USIB) consisted of the director of the CIA, the director of the intelligence bureau at the Department of State (the job that I held), the heads of intelligence in the Departments of the Army, Navy, and Air Force, and representatives from the FBI and the National Security Agency. After the crisis, the Board designated the director of the CIA, the director of intelligence at the Defense Department, and me, the director of intelligence at the State Department, as a subcommittee to conduct a postmortem of the intelligence effort. Our study showed that even after the arms shipments began, of the thousands of refugee reports examined by the intelligence analysts in Washington only eight turned out to be accurate. Five of these refugee reports were of trailers covered with canvas that were so long that the convoy had to stop to remove streetlight posts in order to turn the corners in some of the villages through which they passed. One analyst said later that he "jumped to the conclusion" that these trailers were carrying MRBMs, but did not push his view too hard because no one had been able to lift the canvas and because the repair vehicles for the SAMs were even longer—80 feet.

Few of these reports of long trailers and their difficulties getting around the corners in small villages could be confirmed even by other refugee sightings. Since the practice was that no unconfirmed reports were distributed, neither the analysts preparing the National Intelligence Estimates nor the policy makers were aware of these unconfirmed reports.

However, it is very likely that no harm was done. Such reports served the extraordinarily useful purpose of making the people responsible for gathering intelligence exquisitely sensitive to any kind of information about missiles. On the other hand, even a dozen or so refugee reports confirmed by other refugees would not have been enough evidence for the United States to take the kind of action that was necessary.

Of all the refugee reports two were particularly significant. One, issued by an exile Cuban trade union group, accurately described the Remedios site as it must have looked in mid-September. The second was a very suggestive and accurate description of the early stages of the construction of what became the building at Remedios the Soviets intended to use to store the nuclear warheads. But the first report did not arrive in Washington until October 18, four days after the missiles were discovered by the U–2, and the second did not arrive until October 26, twelve days after the missiles had already been discovered.

Agent reports were of uniformly higher quality than the refugee reports, but they too suffered from a time lag. It took time for a subagent who had observed the unloading of a ship or the movement of a convoy to make his or her way to the master agent, and it took still more time for the master agent to forward the information to the United States. The result was usually a lag of ten days to two weeks between the time something was seen in Cuba and the time the report arrived in Washington.

Another problem was that the number of actual agents with the means for communicating what they saw was very small. They could not be placed randomly around Cuba but had to be sent to places where the probability of seeing something significant was high. And, naturally, these were the places that the Soviets and the Cubans guarded most tightly. As a result, agents actually saw much less activity that suggested missiles than refugees did.

REFUGEES AND SECRET AGENTS

The postmortem study, with the benefit of hindsight, identified only four agent reports, as opposed to refugee reports, that were particularly significant and that arrived in Washington before the missiles were discovered by the U–2.

On September 12, a subagent reported seeing a truck convoy in the middle of the night proceeding in a westerly direction from a secure port area. Included in the convoy were trailers that the agent described as being 20 meters (60 feet) long. However, the contents were concealed by canvas covers stretched over what appeared to be a wooden framework. The report was received in Washington on September 21 and distributed with a CIA headquarters comment to the effect that what the subagent had probably seen was a surface-to-air missile, which is only 30 feet long.

Queried after the crisis, the CIA officials responsible for the comment said that the agent was peeking from behind a drawn curtain in a street that had been restricted because of the movement of war materiel, that the agent was justifiably frightened, and that it was dark. After all, the CIA officials said, the subagent was not able to walk along the trailer with a tape measure, and it seemed highly probable that he had misjudged the length.

A second report received in late September told of Castro's private pilot, drunk in a Havana bar, boasting that Cuba had long-range missiles and no longer feared the United States.

On October 3 and 4 two more agent reports were received in Washington—one of "unusual activity probably connected with missiles" (type not specified) in Pinar del Río, at the western end of Cuba, and a second report that described a second long-trailer convoy seen on September 17, also heading west.

Suggestive though these reports seem to be in hindsight, they were nothing more than suggestive. The U.S. government could hardly crank up a massive effort to blockade Cuba, rally the Latin American governments, and enlist the support of the American people and the NATO Allies on the basis of what a frightened agent thought he saw as he peeked out behind a curtain in the middle of the night, the rantings of a drunken pilot, even though he was Castro's pilot, or two vague reports of long-trailer convoys.

By far the swiftest and most accurate intelligence came from the

U–2 photography. As the world later learned, the whole system—
the camera, the film, and the aircraft itself—was a marvel of design
and engineering. The fuselage of the U–2 was 49 feet, 7 inches, and
the wingspan was 80 feet. The wings were so long that they drooped
when the airspeed dropped on landing and had to be provided with
skids at the wingtips. If the U–2 lost power at altitude, it could glide
for 300 miles.

The advanced Soviet radar deployed in the Soviet Union itself
could detect the U–2. But it made little difference. On the first flight
over the Soviet Union, on July 4, 1956, the Soviets attempted some
20 intercepts with MIG fighters. But their engines flamed out for
lack of oxygen before they got anywhere near the U–2, and they
would arch down like the petals of a flower to an altitude where
they could restart their engines.

A second flight on July 5 went directly over Moscow and its double defensive line of SA–1 surface-to-air antiaircraft missiles without
incident.

At an altitude of 70,000 feet—about 14 miles—pictures were
taken with a resolution that permitted objects 2½ feet square to be
identified. In one memorable photograph of a rocket being fueled at
the Soviet equivalent of Cape Canaveral, the shadow of the umbil-
ical cord feeding fuel into the rocket could be seen. In later years
U–2 pictures were released to the public in which the painted lines
of a parking lot in an American supermarket could be distinguished.
In the hands of skilled photographic interpreters these pictures could
produce an unbelievable amount of extremely accurate information.

Given the accuracy of the U–2 photographs and the uncertainty
of agent and refugee reports, everyone realized that the only intelligence convincing enough to justify the kind of action that would
be needed to remove the Soviet missiles from Cuba would have to
be supplied by the U–2s.

These, then, were the sources of intelligence. But there was also
the problem that Roberta Wohlstetter, in her analysis of the intelligence problem preceding the attack on Pearl Harbor, called the
"noise level"—the hubbub of rumors and false alarms. To intelligence officers, of course, there is nothing new in the problem of
having to separate intelligence bits of sound from a roar of background noise. Roberta Wohlstetter's story of Pearl Harbor "includes
the alarm that fails to work, but also the alarm that has gone off so
often that it has been disconnected"—the cry of "Wolf!" heard so

often that it begins to be ignored. The high command at Pearl Harbor had been alerted to the possibility of a surprise attack on June 17, 1939, on July 25, 1941, and again later that same year on October 16, 1941.[2]

But the history of intelligence failures also includes believing what was actually a *false* alarm. A notable example occurred in World War I. "On August 27," Barbara W. Tuchman wrote in *The Guns of August,* "a seventeen-hour delay in the Liverpool-London railway service inspired the rumor that the trouble was due to the transport of Russian troops who were said to have landed in Scotland on their way to reinforce the Western Front." Fed by nothing more substantial than desperate hope, "the phantoms seen in Scotland took on body, gathering corroborative detail as the story spread." The reports were sometimes ridiculous, but they still succeeded in swaying German intelligence:

> The Russian troops stamped snow off their boots on station platforms—in August; a railway porter of Edinburgh was known to have swept up the snow. "Strange uniforms" were glimpsed in passing troop trains. . . . Ten thousand were seen after midnight in London marching along the Embankment on their way to Victoria Station.

For German intelligence, as often happens, one problem was that the reports were frequently from reliable and respected people.

> An Oxford professor knew a colleague who had been summoned to interpret for them. . . . A resident of Aberdeen, Sir Stuart Coats, wrote to his brother-in-law in America that 125,000 Cossacks had marched across his estate in Perthshire. An English army officer assured friends that 70,000 Russians had passed through England to the Western front in "utmost secrecy."

The effect of these rumors on the Germans was almost as tangible as real Russian troops would have been. "Worry about a possible 70,000 Russians at their back was to be as real a factor at the Marne as the absence of the 70,000 men they had transferred to the Eastern Front."[3]

In the case of Cuba, refugee reports contained much accurate and

useful information about the Soviet arms buildup, but the noise level
was also unusually high. The normal spiraling of rumors was ac-
celerated by a conflict of interest, for the interest of refugees from
Cuba did not always coincide with the interest of the United States.
The best if not the only hope of the Cuban refugees and especially
of the refugee politicians was an American invasion. There was no
need for anyone to manufacture reports, but only to half believe and
pass on the inevitable and completely spontaneous rumors voicing
what most of the refugees so desperately wanted to believe—that
Castro and the Soviets were doing things that made an American
invasion of Cuba necessary for the American national interest and
justifiable before the world.

There were, for example, persistent reports of thousands of uni-
formed Chinese Communists, none of which was ever confirmed.
When the Congo crisis came into the headlines, some of the rumors
from Cuba followed the lead. Near the American base at Guantánamo, according to a number of reports, black African troops had
been seen—some of whom were reported to have rings in their
noses!

The number of reports of missiles in Cuba that were totally without substance numbered in the thousands. For example, the file of
reports devoted solely to missiles in Cuba for the year 1959 is five
inches thick, containing over 3,500 reports—but in 1959 the Soviets
had yet to send arms of any kind to Cuba. Still, some of these reports
were full of persuasive detail. In this 1959 file there are 20 separate
reports pinpointing a "missile installation" in the Ciénaga de Zapata
area, including descriptions of concrete ramps typically associated
with launching pads. Yet the area was in fact an empty swamp and
remains so to this day.

But the stakes were too high for any rumor, no matter how fan-
ciful, to be ignored. Every report containing anything specific that
could be checked against photographs or other intelligence was in
fact checked.

What was also in everyone's mind was the fact that any action
the United States took in Cuba had to be based on evidence that
was not only convincing to the top policy makers in the American
government but also to the American people, to America's Allies,
and to the neutralist members of the UN. Everyone concerned recognized that even the most plausible refugee and agent reports
would probably not be enough to justify military action. The only

intelligence that would really convince the world that the Soviets were putting nuclear missiles in Cuba and justify the kind of action that would be effective against them would have to be supplied by the U–2s.

THE SOVIET BUILDUP

The sources of information available could not by their nature reveal what the Soviets planned to put in Cuba at some future date. But the sources did permit the United States to watch the buildup step-by-step as it proceeded.

The first arms were sent to Cuba in the summer of 1960. On November 18, 1960, the Eisenhower administration announced that at least 12 Soviet ships had delivered arms and ammunition to Cuba and that the total Soviet bloc military aid had so far amounted to about 28,000 tons. Shipments continued intermittently until early 1962, when there was a lull.

The shipments started again in late July, 1962. During the third week in August, it was decided that the United States had enough information to merit giving the press a background briefing, and that I, as the director of intelligence and research at the State Department, should be the one to give it.

The briefing was held on August 24 and catalogued what we knew of the arms buildup so far. It noted that the Soviets had resumed large-scale deliveries of arms to Cuba beginning late in July, after the lull since early 1962; that 8 ships had arrived between July 26 and August 8, and that the total by August 24, at the same time I was speaking, may have reached 20 shiploads.

The cargoes, the briefing continued, included large quantities of transportation, electronic, and construction equipment, such as communications vans, radar vans, trucks, and mobile generator units. The cargoes also included a number of crates that had not yet been opened. Although we did not yet know what was in the crates, we had some suspicions. "From what we have observed of this cargo," the transcript of the briefing reads, "it appears that much of it will go into the improvement of coastal and air defenses. It may include Surface-To-Air Missiles (SAMs), which the Soviets also supplied Iraq and Indonesia."

The briefing noted the arrival of between 3,000 and 5,000 Soviet personnel, many of whom were clearly military technicians, although they did not appear to be in organized combat units but were connected with installing the equipment we had seen coming in and with training Cubans to operate it. None of the Soviets, for example, were in uniform. In fact, not even the Soviets who we later discovered were members of infantry and artillery battle groups wore uniforms. They wore sport shirts and slacks, although the colors and patterns were so limited that it was fairly obvious that the clothing had not been purchased by individuals but issued by some unimaginative quartermaster.

Within 10 days the crates had been opened, revealing surface-to-air missiles. On September 4, President Kennedy released a statement describing what we had seen—antiaircraft missiles similar to our Nike, the radar equipment to operate them, several motor torpedo boats equipped with guided missiles having a range of 15 miles, and 3,500 Soviet military technicians. The president then went on to say:

> There is no evidence of any organized combat force in Cuba from any Soviet bloc country; of military bases provided to Russia; of a violation of the 1934 treaty relating to Guantánamo; of the presence of offensive ground-to-ground missiles; or of other significant offensive capability either in Cuban hands or under Soviet direction and guidance. Were it to be otherwise, the gravest issues would arise.

On September 7, President Kennedy sent a request to Congress for standby authority to call up reserve troops; and on September 11, the Soviet Union in response stated that a U.S. attack on Cuba would mean nuclear war.

Then, on September 13, 1962, the president made a major public statement. Denying any intention to invade Cuba, he went on to issue a warning:

> If at any time the Communist build-up in Cuba were to endanger or interfere with our security in any way, including our base at Guantánamo, our passage to the Panama Canal, our missile and space activities at Cape Canaveral, or the lives of American citizens in this country, or if Cuba should ever attempt to export its aggressive purposes by force or the threat

of force against any nation on this hemisphere, or become an offensive military base of significant capacity for the Soviet Union, then this country will do whatever must be done to protect its own security and that of its allies.

In the meantime, the shuttle of Soviet cargo and passenger ships across the Atlantic continued. And so did American intelligence activities.

A U–2 had covered most of the island on August 29. Another was flown on September 5. The two flights gave an excellent mosaic of the western and central portions of the island, but only spotty coverage of the eastern portion because of cloud cover. What riveted attention was a peculiar installation at the harbor town of Banes, on the northeastern coast.

The installation was a launcher consisting of two rails. It seemed to be designed for a coastal defense role, but it could not be further identified. When the president was briefed, he was annoyed at the ambiguity of the briefers, and said so. This prompted a careful search of the photography that had been taken of Soviet installations worldwide. On September 13, the CIA was able to assure the president that what they had seen was a short-range cruise-missile system with a range of 25 to 30 nautical miles for coastal defense against naval targets.

A second, special flight to look closer at this installation and to cover the rest of the eastern end of the island was delayed for several days by weather, but finally flew on September 26. With considerable relief the intelligence community confirmed that the installation was what they had surmised—a launching platform for a shore-to-ship, cruise-type missile with a range of 25 to 30 miles.

A mission flown on September 17 had produced no usable photographs. The photographs of the missions of August 29, September 5, and September 26, and of a mission on September 29 over the Isle of Pines and the old Bay of Pigs area showed surface-to-air missiles being erected around the perimeter of the island in the western and central portions, additional MIG fighters appearing at various airfields, additional vehicles and supplies for the Cuban ground forces, and several more of the patrol boats armed with short-range missiles. But nothing more.

THE SEPTEMBER 19 NATIONAL INTELLIGENCE ESTIMATE (NIE)

The United States Intelligence Board (USIB) met regularly before and during the crisis. On September 19, 1962, it met for the express purpose of considering the intelligence so far available about the Soviet arms shipments to Cuba. The U–2 photographs revealed no equipment or activity except that described above. No cryptographic or other special intelligence had been received dealing with Cuba. No agent reports had reached Washington of any activity except that already noted, and all refugee reports referring to specific locations had been checked against the available photography. Nothing was identified except the equipment and activity already described.

After deliberation, the USIB noted that the intelligence contained no evidence that the Soviets had sent nuclear missiles to Cuba, and it concluded that on balance they would not do so in the future.

The Board's reasoning was as follows. First, the Soviets must have realized that because of the massive Soviet arms shipments to Cuba the United States would be flying the U–2 over Cuba regularly and that the likelihood of discovery was therefore high. Second, the Soviets must have realized that if they sent missiles to Cuba, the United States would probably react strongly. Third, although the problem of Soviet strategic inferiority would be eased by sending missiles to Cuba, it would not be solved. Fourth, the Soviets had never in the past sent nuclear weapons outside their own borders, even to the Eastern European satellites. Finally, Castro was a self-elected member of the Communist bloc, which ran counter to Soviet conceptions of themselves and their world, and the Soviets were not likely to regard him as trustworthy. Castro and his regime were also regarded as unstable.

So the unanimous judgment of the Intelligence Board was that the Soviets would *not* deploy nuclear missiles in Cuba. The operational paragraph, which has been declassified, is as follows:

D. The USSR could derive considerable military advantage from the establishment of Soviet medium and intermediate range ballistic missiles in Cuba, or from the establishment of a Soviet submarine base there. As between these two, the establishment of a submarine base would be the more likely. Either development, however, would be incompatible with Soviet practice to date and with Soviet policy as we presently estimate it. It would indicate a far greater willingness to increase the level of risk in US-Soviet relations than the USSR has displayed thus far, and consequently would have important policy implications with respect to other areas and other problems in East-West relations. (Paras. 29–33)[4]

However, the hedge that the "USSR could derive considerable military advantage from the establishment of Soviet medium and intermediate range ballistic missiles in Cuba," contained in the NIE that the USIB approved, increased the considerable uneasiness felt throughout the intelligence community, for the obvious reason that the possible gains were large enough to be tempting for the Soviets. Although it was hardly necessary, the intelligence community was cautioned to maintain a high state of alert.

John McCone, the director of central intelligence, was on a honeymoon trip in Europe and did not attend the meeting. However, a month later it transpired that he had been briefed at one of the American embassies by the CIA station chief on the CIA draft of the estimate and that he had cabled to express doubts about the conclusion that the Soviets would not put missiles in Cuba. The members of the USIB also learned that even earlier, in August, in a conversation with President Kennedy about Soviet motives in putting the SAM antiaircraft missiles in Cuba, McCone had speculated that the purpose of the SAMs might be to screen the introduction of offensive missiles rather than to defend Cuba against a possible invasion.

Thirty years later, on October 19, 1992, the CIA held a public conference on the anniversary of the missile crisis, and the conferees were supplied with a number of documents that had been declassified.[5] Among them were a large number of internal CIA memos from McCone repeating again and again his suspicions that the Soviets intended to put nuclear missiles in Cuba.

McCone's reasoning was that the Soviets could not really believe that antiaircraft missiles and the other equipment they were giving the Cubans would actually stop the United States from invading Cuba if it wanted to, and that the Soviets must have a more important motive for putting the SAMs in Cuba—to shoot down our reconnaissance U–2s and prevent us from discovering offensive missiles.

The CIA estimators argued in their return cable that the available facts also fitted a more conservative explanation. The SAM weapons in Cuba were the advanced version, the SA–2, which was the same missile that had shot down Gary Powers. The Soviets were rightly proud of the weapon, and they had been deploying it with a free hand, even providing it to both Iraq and Indonesia.

Furthermore, given the Bay of Pigs affair of the year before, the estimators argued, the Soviets probably thought that Castro's fear of invasion was justifiable. Even if the Soviets did not believe it themselves, giving Castro the weapons to counter an invasion would ensure Castro's gratitude.

Finally, the estimators pointed out, arms aid including antiaircraft missiles would at least guarantee that the United States could not pretend that exile groups were responsible for any future invasion but would have to take the public onus of doing the job itself.

The argument was persuasive, but when McCone was cabled the final conclusion of the September 19 estimate, he cabled back urging a most careful consideration of the conclusion that the introduction of offensive missiles was unlikely. But the estimate had already been endorsed by the USIB and released.

McCone often played the devil's advocate in arguing with the CIA estimators, but this time he was arguing from conviction. Although he had no evidence, hard or soft, he had a gut feeling that the Soviets intended to put offensive missiles in Cuba—based solely on his deep suspicion of the Soviets and their motives. As McCone himself said later, "Let me make it unmistakably clear that there was no—I repeat no—hard evidence supporting my view in August that there were offensive missiles going into Cuba. It was wholly a question of judgment."[6]

U–2 DIFFICULTIES

In the meantime the intelligence-gathering effort was having difficulties. If the weather was right a U–2 could cover the whole island of Cuba in a single flight. As a practical matter, however, there was usually some cloud cover, and for some time the routine had been to have two U–2 flights a month.

The August 29 flight went up one side of a line drawn down the middle of the island and down the other in the usual pattern designed to give a mosaic of the whole island in a single trip. The September 5 flight concentrated on the eastern and central parts of the island.

The next scheduled flight was to repeat the pattern of the August 29 flight, up one side of the island and down the other. But the rapid deployment of the SAMs and the fact that they were the more advanced type caused some second thoughts.

Many people in the Air Force and some in the CIA argued that a Soviet SAM could not shoot down a U–2 at full altitude—that when Gary Powers was shot down over the Soviet Union, it must have been because engine trouble had brought him to a lower altitude within range. But there were solid doubts about this somewhat parochial thesis, and no one wanted to risk a pilot's life needlessly or to raise an international political storm that might restrict the flights in some way similar to the limitations forced on Eisenhower after Gary Powers was shot down. Without the U–2, American intelligence would be blinded.

Then, as if to underline both points, two U–2 incidents occurred in rapid succession on the other side of the world. On September 7, a U–2 accidentally violated Soviet airspace over Sakhalin. It was picked up by radar and chased by Soviet fighters, but escaped. Then on September 10 a Chinese Nationalist U–2 was shot down over mainland China.

The next day the group that normally considered such matters, with the addition of the secretary of state, Dean Rusk, met in McGeorge Bundy's office in the west basement of the White House. It was quickly agreed that the U–2 flights should continue, but it was also agreed that the usual flight pattern should be altered to minimize the risk of a shoot-down.

Dean Rusk suggested, first, that rather than a single flight that would keep the U–2 over Cuba for a long period of time, there should be several flights that "dipped into" Cuban airspace. In addition, he suggested that these actual overflights should be obscured by a very large number of peripheral flights that looked into Cuba on the slant while remaining outside the three-mile limit. The idea seemed to be a good solution to the problem, and it was this proposal that was adopted.

Although the group may not have been made aware of it, the

decision upset the photo interpreters because slant photographs taken from outside the international limit could see only 25 miles into Cuba, and therefore failed to cover a large portion of the center of the island.

For the remainder of September attention in the intelligence community continued to focus mainly on the eastern end of the island. As mentioned above, the special flight to look at Banes finally flew on September 26.[7]

Reports of "unusual activity" on the Isle of Pines and the old Bay of Pigs area caused a flurry in late September, and a U–2 was flown over both places on September 29. The activity was revealed as the installation of a SAM and another of the short-range coastal defense missiles first identified at Banes. Following this, there was still some residual worry about the eastern end of the island, and a U–2 was sent there on a peripheral flight on October 5 and another on October 7.

Then there were the agent reports already discussed—the agent report of a trailer 60 feet long that CIA headquarters thought was only 30, the boasting of Castro's pilot, and the vague reports of long-trailer convoys. Suggestive though these reports now seem to be, to repeat the arguments given above, they were nothing more than suggestive. These reports had neither more nor less impact than similar reports received in the past. The intelligence community had been worried that the Soviets might put missiles in Cuba from the beginning of the arms buildup. These worries continued in spite of the conclusion of the September 19 NIE that they probably would not. The community was also worried about the possibility of a submarine base, installations that might interfere with our space work at Cape Canaveral, and about Cuban-based subversion—and also about the possibility that the Soviets might do something no one had even thought of.

The policy makers were also worried. As already noted, President Kennedy issued a series of public warnings to the Soviets against putting offensive weapons in Cuba. Very early he recognized that if the Soviets did put missiles in Cuba, he would need time to work out a response. Therefore he instituted the special Psalm security clearance restricting information about "offensive weapons" in Cuba to those who would need to know to do their jobs in both the intelligence and policy-making communities.

However, even though reports of the kind described above were hardly justification for starting a war, they did have an extremely important impact. In spite of the CIA headquarters' comment downgrading the first report about a trailer 60 feet long, for example, in the secretary of state's morning staff meeting I had specifically called everyone's special attention to the report—taking the unusual step of reading the whole report aloud.

But even though the vague allegations in these reports did not provide the basis for taking action against Cuba, they did increase everyone's sensitivity—and nervousness. But the truth is that everyone's antennae were already quivering, that they had been quivering for weeks, and that the tension in the intelligence community, the Pentagon, the State Department, and the White House was extreme.

In late September the specific worry had been about the portion of the eastern end of the island still hidden under clouds. The first two flights in October, to repeat, were scheduled to inspect the eastern and not the western end of the island. Thin and tenuous as the agent and refugee reports were, these reports triggered no special intelligence estimate. But they did focus attention again on the western end of the island, where some kind of activity, it now seemed clear, was going on. It was to consider flights over the western end of the island that a special meeting was held on October 4. The agent reports described above were not mentioned at the meeting, but McCone brought with him a map of Cuba showing what areas had been covered by which flights and the CIA's estimate as to which of the antiaircraft SAMs were most advanced in their construction.

The map showed that a trapezoidal area (which covered, as later turned out, both San Cristóbal and Guanajay) had not been covered since September 5; it was in this area that the SAMs were most advanced. It was perfectly obvious that if missiles had been deployed to Cuba they would have to be in this region, since all the others had been photographed and found empty. The discussion focused on how soon the antiaircraft SAMs would be operational, the risk to the U–2 pilot, and the continued use of the U–2 as an intelligence source.[8]

The dilemma between the need to continue intelligence surveillance of the island and the danger to the U–2 had led me several days earlier, late in September, to suggest redirecting the satellites, which were programmed to cover the Soviet Union, to fly over Cuba. But the idea was quickly discarded when we discovered that re-scheduling the satellites would mean a substantial delay.

The increasing danger of losing a U–2 also prompted a dispute between the Pentagon and the CIA. On the grounds that if a U–2 was shot down it would be better to have the pilot be a regular officer in uniform, McNamara succeeded in having the Air Force take over in spite of the CIA's hotly argued protest that the CIA planes were better equipped with protective devices. The solution was to let Air Force pilots fly the CIA U–2s, but the dispute cost another day or two delay.

At the October 4 meeting, it was decided to instruct those charged with U–2 operations to prepare for the group's further consideration a flight plan that would slice across the western end of the island through the middle of the trapezoid and come near enough to the most advanced SAM site to photograph it but not near enough to be shot down. Working out the flight plan caused another slight delay, and on October 9, the special group met again and approved the plan that had been prepared.

THE POLITICAL PROBLEM

The rest of official Washington in the meantime was faced with a political problem which they dealt with as best they could, continuing to make public the information on the buildup as it was confirmed. On October 3, George W. Ball, the undersecretary of state, testified before a congressional committee in an open hearing on trade with Cuba. His statement, which was prepared from the daily CIA and Defense Intelligence Agency summaries and which I personally cleared with John McCone on October 2, gave the situation as we then knew it. Eighty-five shiploads of armaments had arrived in Cuba; 15 antiaircraft SAM sites had been established, and a total of 25 was predicted. Four coastal defense missile sites, 60 older-type MIGs, at least 1 advanced-type MIG 21, 16 missile patrol boats, and about 4,500 Soviet technicians had been identified in Cuba.

When the committee chairman asked about the reliability of the intelligence and whether Cuba was becoming an offensive base, Ball replied that our information, we believed, was "quite complete." He then continued:

Our intelligence is very good and very hard. All the indications are that this is equipment which is basically of a defensive capability, and that it does not offer any offensive capabilities to Cuba as against the United States or the other nations of the hemisphere.

SENATOR KEATING'S INTERVENTION

Senator Kenneth B. Keating and Senator Barry Goldwater, both Republicans, had tried for some time to make whatever political hay they could out of the Cuban situation. Senator Keating was especially active. After the news stories based on my background briefing of the press on August 24, for example, Keating made a speech in the Senate repeating the basic information I had provided, with three differences. First, he called the Soviet personnel in Cuba "troops" rather than "technicians." Second, he said they were wearing uniforms. Third, he failed to say that the rest of his information had come from a State Department briefing, leaving the impression that he had somehow discovered all this information by himself.

The State Department denied that there was any information that the Soviet personnel were "troops"—meaning organized fighting units—rather than technicians or that they were wearing uniforms. After the crisis this statement gave Keating the excuse to imply that everything he had said had been denied, when in fact everything he said, except for the claims about troops and uniforms, had come straight from my background briefing of the press.[9]

Keating made several such speeches on the Senate floor between August 31 and October 1, none of which ever went any further than the official State Department press backgrounders, except for such points as whether the Soviets wore uniforms or whether they should correctly be called troops or technicians. The only other difference was that Keating kept calling for "action"—although he never specified just what the action should be.

On October 9, just a few days after George Ball's testimony, Keating again took to the floor and again confined himself largely to what Ball had already made public.

Then, only 24 hours later, on October 10, Keating appeared on the floor in something of a rush and made another speech on Cuba. But this time he did say something different from what was in the backgrounders. He charged that six IRBM bases were being constructed in Cuba.

After the crisis was over, Keating apparently began to fear that he was vulnerable to the charge that he had either been peddling refugee rumors or that he had failed to give the U.S. government information vital to national security that he alone possessed. For he began to insist, first, that the information he had was not mere refugee rumor and, second, that it was already known to the government.

In an interview on the NBC program *Monitor* on Sunday, November 4, he said:

> on the tenth day of October I said that there were six intermediate missile sites under construction in Cuba. . . . That was denied. . . . And I want to say right here and now, that at every time when I spoke on this subject I either had it from official sources or I had it from others and confirmed by official sources before I ever said a word.

The senator elaborated on the theme in an interview with *U.S. News and World Report* published on November 19, 1962:

> Q. Senator, what were the sources of your information about Cuba?
>
> A. The sources were either (a) sources in the U.S. government or (b) other sources—less than 5 per cent of which were Cuban refugees—all of which were verified through official sources of the U.S. government before I made my statement . . .
>
> Q. What about the intermediate range missiles—those with a range of more than 2000 miles?
>
> A. The intermediate missile launching sites came to my attention in early October. This information was verified officially on October 9, and I spoke on October 10.

With which "official" Senator Keating "verified" this information remains a mystery. The senator refused to name his source, other than to say it was an "American" who had "access to reliable information." Much later, in 1964, Keating elaborated:

It was inconceivable to me that high officials would be in the dark over such a large-scale and important development. Yet it is clear now that they were.

Since no one in the intelligence community knew that there were missiles in Cuba until after October 14, it is difficult to see how the senator could have "verified" the information with any American official. In actuality, as soon as Senator Keating's charges began to come over the tickers on October 10, Thomas L. Hughes, deputy director of intelligence and research at the State Department, personally telephoned the chief of every intelligence agency in Washington or one of his deputies to ask if any of them had any reports to which Senator Keating might be referring. The answers were uniformly negative, and the State Department so informed the press.

If Keating's claim was correct that his source was lower down in the government and that the source had not informed his superior officers, then the source was certainly guilty of dereliction of duty by concealing vital information from his superiors—and possibly of treason. But Keating steadfastly refused to identify his source. Indeed, Keating went to his grave without ever doing so.

If the first mystery is where Keating got his information, the second is just what information he had. Keating said there were six intermediate-range missile sites in Cuba, but he did not say where they were located. If he knew, he was withholding information that was vital to the United States; if he did not know the locations, how did he come by the figure six?

One of the most puzzling aspects of Keating's claim, in fact, is the use of this exact number—six sites, not "a number of sites" or "a site." In fact, the Soviets intended to build *four* intermediate-range missile sites and *six* medium-range sites. But we now know that at the time Keating was speaking construction was not far enough along on several of the sites for even an expert to have recognized them as missile sites, much less a refugee or an ordinary secret agent. The implication of an exact number, such as six, is that the information came from one of three sources. One possibility would be an intelligence research organization which received and compared different reports, checking one against the other and reaching a conclusion on the total number of separate sites. The second possibility would be a high official of either the Soviet or Cuban government. The third possibility is that the information was in fact false but that someone wanted to lend authenticity to a deliberate plant of false information by making it appear that the story came from either an intelligence organization or a high-level official in the Cuban or Soviet governments.

It might be argued that Keating got some refugee reports before official Washington did and served as his own intelligence research organization. But there were no reports that came to the intelligence community later and reported "six intermediate-range missile sites" or that were available at the time that could have been totaled up to six sites.

There seem to be, in fact, only two refugee reports of any significance that Keating might have gotten before official Washington did, but neither of these reports corresponds to Keating's allegations. The report describing the Remedios site as of mid-September, to repeat, was issued by an exile Cuban trade union group on October 18—which was four days after the missiles were discovered by the U–2. The other, describing construction of what became the building the Soviets intended to use to store the warheads at Remedios, did not arrive in Washington until October 26, 12 days after the missiles were discovered by the U–2. But both of these reports described one site, not six.

As to the possibility that someone in the top levels of the Cuban or Soviet governments disagreed with the decision to permit the Soviets to deploy missiles in Cuba and was discreetly trying to warn the United States, the U.S. government had no such source.

The only incident that even remotely suggests that a high Cuban or Soviet official was trying to warn the United States was a peculiarly elliptical statement by President Osvaldo Dorticós of Cuba in an address before the UN General Assembly. On October 8, 1962, Dorticós said, ". . . we have sufficient means with which to defend ourselves; we have indeed our unavoidable weapons, the weapons which we would have preferred not to acquire and which we do not wish to employ." What makes this explanation conceivable is that the Spanish word *inevitable,* which Dorticós used, may be translated as "fatal" as well as "unavoidable."

But if Dorticós or some other Cuban or Soviet official chose Senator Keating to be the channel for transmitting more specific information, the choice seems incredibly bizarre. But even so the mystery would still remain, not only why Keating refused even after the crisis was long over to reveal his source, but also why he kept insisting that he had "confirmed" the information with sources inside the U.S. government.

On balance it seems much more likely that Dorticós was not attempting to inform anyone about missiles in Cuba but merely attempting to warn the United States, the CIA, or anyone else that Cuba was prepared to fight.

So the most likely explanation of Keating's information and his refusal to say anything about his source was that in a time of extreme national danger he either acted for his own personal political advantage or let himself be rushed into peddling what were either rumors or a deliberate plant of false information put out by Cuban exiles whose interest was to push the United States into an invasion.

The simple fact remains that the responsible officials of the U.S. government had no information—from either intelligence or Senator Keating—that permitted them to conclude that the Soviets had put missiles in Cuba or were going to.

Thus it was that McGeorge Bundy, President Kennedy's national security adviser, appearing on ABC's *Issues and Answers* on Sunday, October 14, denied that the U.S. government had any information about missiles in Cuba. Asked specifically about offensive weapons in Cuba, Bundy said:

Well, I don't myself think that there is any present—I *know* there is no present evidence, and I think there is no present likelihood that the Cubans and the Cuban government and the Soviet government would in combination attempt to install a major offensive capability. It is true that the MIG fighters which have been put in Cuba for more than a year now, and any possible additions in the form of aircraft, might have a certain marginal capability for moving against the United States. But I think we have to bear in mind the relative magnitudes. The United States is not going to be placed in any position of major danger to its own security by Cuba, and we are not going to permit that situation to develop. . . . So far, everything that has been delivered in Cuba falls within the categories of aid which the Soviet Union has provided, for example, to neutral states like Egypt or Indonesia, and I should not be surprised to see additional military assistance of that sort.

In referring to "possible additions in the form of aircraft" and to "categories of aid which the Soviet Union has provided, for example, to neutral states like Egypt or Indonesia," Bundy had in his mind the U–2 pictures, already mentioned, of crates being unloaded in Cuba of a very peculiar shape that had been used to ship IL–28s to Egypt and Indonesia. Later U–2 pictures confirmed that the crates photographed in Cuba did in fact contain IL–28s.

However, the same day that Bundy was appearing on TV, October 14, 1962, the ubiquitous U–2 was about to lift the curtain. On October 9, 1962, a U–2 flight was approved at the highest level and was readied on October 10. It stood by, waiting for a prediction for good weather on October 11, 12, and 13.

On Sunday, October 14, the flight was made as planned and without incident. Routinely, the package of films was flown to the processing laboratories that night. Routinely, the processed film was flown to the photointerpretation center Monday morning, October 15. Routinely, the photointerpreters began going over the pictures, frame by frame.

Then, suddenly, routine stopped. At San Cristóbal, in western Cuba, the photographs clearly showed the erector launchers, missile-carrying trailers, fueling trucks, and radar vans of a battalion of Soviet medium-range ballistic missiles.

NOTES

1. Two other, even more sensitive sources, electronic intelligence ("Elint") and code breaking, did not play an important role in this early part of the Cuban missile crisis. "Elint" does not play a large role in tracking ships at sea, and either the Soviets did not use electronic forms of communication about the missiles or they used codes that the United States had not succeeded in breaking.

2. Roberta Wohlstetter, *Pearl Harbor: Warning and Decision* (Stanford, CA: Stanford University Press, 1962), Chapter 2, *passim.*

3. Barbara W. Tuchman, *The Guns of August* (New York: Macmillan, 1962), pp. 388–90.

4. Mary S. McAuliffe, ed., *CIA Documents on the Cuban Missile Crisis, 1962* (Washington, DC: History Staff, Central Intelligence Agency, October, 1992).

5. Ibid.

6. Thomas L. Hughes, *The Fate of Facts in a World of Men: Foreign Policy and Intelligence-Making* (New York: The Foreign Policy Association, Headline Series No. 233, 1976), p. 44.

7. In the aftermath of the Cuban crisis, a newspaper reporter noted a discrepancy in delays attributed to cloud cover and the actual weather conditions over Cuba during the period. But it was not *actual* weather that determined whether a flight would or would not go, but the *predicted* weather. If the predicted weather was for less than 50 percent cloud cover, the flight would go. If the predicted weather was for more than 50 percent, the flight was usually delayed. But the weather did not always turn out to be as predicted.

8. Both Colonel John Ralph Wright, Jr., of the Defense Intelligence Agency, and Navy Captain Charles R. Clark were later credited with suggesting that the San Cristóbal–Guanajay area was a likely missile site.

9. The fact that there were four combat groups of Soviet troops in Cuba was not discovered until low-level reconnaissance permitted them to be identified, and low-level reconnaissance was not authorized until after the crisis had become public. Even in President Kennedy's October 22 speech, he referred to "Soviet technicians" rather than "troops" because we had no information that would indicate they were anything but technicians.

Chapter 3

The Intelligence Postmortem

From the Soviet point of view, what had gone wrong? Jumping ahead, the most serious error the Soviets made was in their estimate of the probable American response. It has been suggested that the Soviets underestimated the U.S. response for two reasons. First, the Soviets thought that the democracies were "too liberal to fight," as the poet Robert Frost reported Khrushchev as saying. On the other hand, as Arthur M. Schlesinger, Jr., has pointed out, Frost was interpreting an anecdote Khrushchev had quoted from Gorki, and Frost distorted Khrushchev's meaning in the process.[1]

It has been suggested, second, that Khrushchev was accustomed to people who blustered, and Kennedy's mild behavior at the Vienna meeting and his refusal to use American troops at the Bay of Pigs led Khrushchev to conclude that Kennedy was an inexperienced leader who could be threatened and bluffed into acquiescence. But both the Bay of Pigs and the Vienna meeting had come a year earlier, and since that time Kennedy had done a number of things that would have demonstrated his toughness to Khrushchev, including standing firm on Berlin and putting troops in Thailand when the Communist side in Laos broke the cease-fire.

So it seems more likely that the Soviet decision depended on much more than one man's estimate of another. The more likely cause of the Soviet leadership's failure to foresee the level of the American reaction runs much deeper, rooted in fundamental cultural and historical differences that colored their judgments.

American attitudes toward Latin America, particularly Cuba, derive from an intimate history, which the Soviets seem not to have fully appreciated. Then, too, Americans came to nationhood behind the protective moat of two oceans, and one of the proudest principles of their foreign policy was the Monroe Doctrine, which had declared the entire hemisphere off-limits to European powers. So the first major intrusion of foreign military power into the Western Hemisphere in modern times was to have a shock effect that the Soviets could not easily understand. After all, on the European continent enemies are just the other side of a land or river border.

It may also be that American attitudes were so deeply held that the Americans themselves failed to recognize the need to articulate and explain them and thus from 1959 to 1962 sent out inadequate or even false signals that contributed to the Soviet misunderstanding.

Finally, it is very clear that Communist ideology distorted the Soviets' view of the world and handicapped them in understanding the attitudes and motivations of other peoples, especially, perhaps, Americans.

In any case, of the whole range of possible American responses to their putting missiles in Cuba, the Soviets apparently thought that only two were likely: (1) the United States would protest loudly, appeal to the UN, but ultimately acquiesce even though its strategic advantage had been sharply reduced; or (2) the United States would first threaten, but then sit down to negotiate—and the negotiations might include, if the balance of forces was favorable to the Soviets, the subject the Soviets had foremost on their agenda, Berlin.

This is not to say that the Soviets thought the Cuba venture was without risk. But it does indicate that they thought of it as an easily manageable risk. As it turned out, the risk *was* manageable; the error was thinking that managing it would be easy.

It could be argued, of course, that a second Soviet mistake was in getting caught—or at least in getting caught before the missile force was operational. If all the missiles, both the MRBMs and the IRBMs, had been discovered only after they were all fully operational, the U.S. response may well have been the same—as I personally believe both that it would have been and that it should have been. But with all the missiles fully in place and operational, the Soviet bargaining position would have been at least *somewhat* better than it was with only the MRBMs in place and ready to fire.

One possible explanation is that something went wrong in the mechanics of the deployment. If one assumes that the antiaircraft SAMs were intended to screen the installation of the offensive missiles, then they should have been in place and operational before the first of the long-range missiles and missile-associated equipment arrived—and if necessary used to shoot down American planes. In fact, however, the SAMs and their associated radar nets did not become operational as a system until about October 27, when the U–2 was shot down, or at most a day or two earlier.

We know that there were some technical difficulties—drainage problems, for example—that made it necessary to relocate at least some of the SAMs. But to screen the installation of the missiles, the SAMs would have to have been operational at the latest by October 1, as we shall see, and possibly as much as two weeks earlier. So it seems doubtful that technical difficulties could have caused a whole month's delay.

The Soviets relied on speed rather than camouflage when the missiles arrived at the sites, and the best explanation may be that they intended to substitute speed for screening by the SAMs, too. Using the SAMs as a screen would have meant shooting down U.S. reconnaissance flights and thus heating up Soviet-American relations before the Soviets were ready for a confrontation. Recognizing this, the Soviets may have intended to use the SAMs not to screen the installation of the missiles but to remove any temptation the Americans might have felt to try to take the missiles out by selective air strikes. The State Department's frequent background briefings of the press and the accurate accounts in the American newspapers day by day as the equipment went into Cuba would certainly have left the Soviets in no doubt that the United States was conducting U–2 reconnaissance.

Somewhat later the Soviets should have drawn the same conclusion from Bowles' hammering on "offensive weapons" in his conversation with Dobrynin and the president's pointedly reading Gromyko his earlier warnings about putting missiles in Cuba. Both incidents suggested not only that the United States was conducting a vigorous campaign of U–2 reconnaissance, but that the United States had already found out about the missiles.

Since the Soviets had learned all about the capabilities of the

U–2 when they shot down Gary Powers, it seems unlikely that they did not realize how good the American reconnaissance was. But it is conceivable the Soviets concluded that they didn't really need to make the effort to get the SAMs ready because they really didn't need to run the risk of shooting down an American U–2. After all, if the combination of secrecy first and then speed did not work, the Americans were not expected to react violently anyway.

U.S. INTELLIGENCE

What about the American intelligence effort? Was it a success or a failure? Could the missiles have been discovered any earlier than they were?

Flights on August 29 and September 5 showed nothing at all at San Cristóbal, Remedios, or Sagua la Grande, and only some unidentifiable scratchings of the earth at Guanajay. But the October 14 flight and others in the days immediately following October 14 showed some sites that were recognizable as ballistic missile installations in all four areas.

Survey work for the MRBM and IRBM sites must have been done in July or August. Construction work was apparently started on the Guanajay IRBM site in early September. On the San Cristóbal and Remedios sites work started sometime between September 15 and September 20. On the Sagua la Grande site work began sometime between September 25 and September 30.

As to missiles and missile-related equipment, in the aftermath of the crisis we came to believe that the first missile shipment had probably arrived in Cuba on September 8, and that the equipment was then moved out to the sites by night convoys—probably between September 9 and September 14, since the agent's sighting of the convoy with what he described as 60-foot trailers was on September 12. We also believed that the second shipment probably arrived on September 15, again with the convoys moving out over the next few days.

From the time the Soviet decision to deploy missiles to Cuba was made in June until the missiles were actually installed, classic methods of intelligence—that is, old-fashioned espionage—might have provided information of the Soviet intention to put missiles in Cuba if an agent had penetrated the inner circle of the Kremlin or Castro's immediate entourage. This, of course, did not happen, and in the history of nations it rarely has.[2]

In the second stage—from sometime in September, when the missiles arrived at the ports, until the time they were installed at the sites—classic spying might have even revealed the actual presence of the missiles. An agent did in fact see a convoy and report unusually long trailers, as we have seen. But he was not able to peek under the canvas covering the trailers, which theoretically could have been done by an agent among the Soviet troops that unloaded the equipment and drove the convoys or among those few Cuban soldiers who were used as guides, guards, or liaison officers.

But notice, first, that the classic methods of espionage are extraordinarily difficult, time-consuming, and risky. Not obtaining information by classic means should not necessarily be counted a failure, while getting it would have been a lucky break. And notice, secondly, that to take the action the United States did in fact take and to mobilize public opinion in the United States and among our Allies to support that action required "harder" information than agent reports. It was only in the third stage—after missiles and supporting equipment had actually been installed at the launching sites—that the necessary hard information could be acquired. The hardest information of all were pictures, and it was only in this third stage that the installations would be recognizable in aerial photography.

The United States, in other words, could not have reasonably expected to get the kind of information it needed until this third stage, when the missiles and related equipment began to appear at the sites. But when did this stage begin?

In the period following October 14, U–2s flew several times a day, and intelligence was able to watch the progress of construction on several of the sites almost hour by hour. The "before and after" pictures we were able to take of some of the sites of the 1,000-mile MRBMs that were not started until after October 14 make it possible to construct an extremely accurate timetable.

The MRBMs were a mobile, "field-type" missile. Designed for use by ground forces in combat, they were very similar to heavy artillery battalions in the way they were transported and put into position. They required no fixed installations, no concrete ramps, control bunkers, or launching pads. All they needed was a dirt approach road and a flat piece of ground big enough to back together two vehicles—a missile trailer bringing the missile to where it was to be erected and a missile erector to lift the missile to an upright position. As Secretary McNamara testified, these highly mobile, 1,000-mile *medium-range* missiles could be "deactivated, moved, reactivated on a new site, and ready for operations within a period of about six days."

From the time the MRBMs arrived at a new location, in other words, they could in a pinch be put into operation within 72 hours. Working backward from this, the CIA concluded—and so testified before the Preparedness Subcommittee of the Senate's Armed Services Committee—that the earliest an MRBM site for launching the 1,000-mile missile could have been identified from the air was October 8.

The 2,000-mile IRBMs were different. They *did* require permanent construction. It was the four-slash "signature" of excavation for concrete revetments and associated equipment that revealed that the Soviets intended to put the 2,000-mile *intermediate-range* missiles into Cuba, for, so far as we know, no IRBM missiles ever arrived in Cuba. The missiles we actually saw at the sites inside Cuba and on the ships going out were MRBMs. In fact, the 2,000-mile IRBM sites, which were not scheduled for completion until mid-November, never did reach a stage where they were ready to receive the missiles themselves. As already mentioned, what permitted us to recognize the IRBM sites were the characteristic four slashes on the ground, the concrete bunkers going up, the concrete flash deflectors, the storage sites being constructed that were typical of those used for nuclear warheads, and other, associated equipment.

The truth of the matter is that no one really knows just when this construction could have first been recognized as an IRBM site. None of the missile sites was recognizable as such on the August 29 and September 5 U-2 flights; some were recognizable on the October 14 flight. The refugee whose report did not arrive in Washington until October 26 saw construction in mid-September that later, with the benefit of hindsight, seems suggestive. But whether the construction he saw would have been recognizable from the air as a missile site in mid-September is questionable.

If one wishes to consider a nightmare scenario, suppose a U-2 had flown over the sites on September 15, and construction at that time had not been far enough along to recognize anything significant. The United States might have been lulled into starting once more at the other end of the island and not gotten around to the fateful trapezoid until very late in October or even early November!

It could reasonably be argued that the U–2 flight of October 14 found the missiles at just about the earliest possible date, especially considering the fact that the plane was standing by to fly on the 11th, the 12th, and the 13th and was delayed because of the predictions of unfavorable weather.

On the other hand, it could also be argued that if the intelligence community had gotten suspicious of the western end of the island in late September and dispatched a U–2 to the right spot on, say, October 2 or 3, it might well have come back with the photographic proof. A day or two might also have been saved if the job of plotting a route for the October 14 flight that dodged the SAMs had been done with more dispatch. And a day or two would probably have been saved if the Air Force and the CIA had been less bureaucratic about who would fly the plane.

The question is whether it is reasonable to conclude that the intelligence community should have had its suspicions aroused about the western end of the island sooner than it did. There was no hint of location in the braggings of Castro's pilot, and therefore nothing to check. It is understandable that the CIA was skeptical of the single agent's estimate of the length of a moving trailer observed at night under difficult and nerve-wracking circumstances—especially when one considers the background noise and mass of similar reports that had been proved false. Even so, it is not unreasonable to say that the *first* report of a convoy *heading west* with what appeared to be exceptionally long trailers should have aroused more suspicion than it did.[3]

I, for one, was even more willing to subscribe to this criticism when I later discovered that it was skepticism and skepticism alone that had prompted the CIA headquarters comment that what the agent had seen was probably a 30-foot SAM antiaircraft missile. For I had assumed that the comment was put in for technical reasons— because, for example, the truck was not big enough to pull that kind of trailer, or some such.

Something else that was overlooked at the time, however, seems even more suggestive when one is armed with hindsight. In going back over the reports, it was discovered that two of the Soviet cargo ships diverted from their normal tasks to carry arms to Cuba—the

Omsk and the *Poltava*—had exceptionally large hatches. Looking back, the intelligence experts concluded that it was these large-hatch ships that had brought in the 60-foot medium-range missiles in such secrecy. When the missiles were returned to the Soviet Union they were carried on the decks of ordinary freighters and covered with canvas for protection from the weather. But none of the pictures of ships going into Cuba showed such deck cargo.

What was also significant in hindsight was not only that these ships had large hatches but the fact that the intelligence reports also routinely noted that they were riding high in the water—indicating that they were carrying "space-consuming" cargo of low weight and high volume.

But neither the fact that these ships had exceptionally large hatches nor that they were carrying space-consuming cargo was brought to the attention of either the policy makers or the top levels of the intelligence agencies until after the missiles had been discovered in Cuba.

It is not too difficult to understand why the professional intelligence technicians down the line failed to see enough significance in these facts to bring them to the attention of the top levels. There was nothing new or startling about the ships themselves. One of the ships, the *Omsk,* had been built in Japan, and the CIA told us in the aftermath of the crisis that both had been specially designed for the Soviet lumbering industry, where extra-large hatches are necessary and normal—although it turned out that the ships had actually been designed with large hatches for more general purposes. Also, it was known that the Soviets had had some trouble finding the ships they needed to send their military aid to Cuba, and the intelligence specialists on shipping presumably thought it was understandable that the large-hatch ships could be more easily spared than some other kinds.

Roberta Wohlstetter, pursuing her interest in the intelligence problem that she had begun with her analysis of the attack on Pearl Harbor, saw this failure to notice the possible significance of the large-hatch ships as an attempt to "save" a theory—the theory that the Soviets would not put missiles into Cuba—by explaining away disturbing or unusual observations.[4] But the point here is just the opposite: The shipping intelligence specialists did not see the facts that the ships had large hatches and that they were riding high in the water as unusual or disturbing enough even to call attention to them, much less explain them away. The explanations came much later, when the discovery of the missiles caused a formal postmortem to try to reconstruct what had happened and when.

In any case, it was not until the September 19 estimate that the intelligence community addressed itself to the question of whether the Soviets would put missiles into Cuba, and the shipping specialists did not know what the "Sovietologists" thought the Soviets would do until after that September 19 estimate was distributed, several days later.

It was, I believe, clearly an intelligence failure that these facts about the large-hatch ships and their riding high in the water was not called to the special attention of the people at the top of the intelligence agencies and the policy makers in the State Department, the Defense Department, and the White House. But it seems to me that it was a failure not of rationalization, of explaining away the obvious, as Wohlstetter would have it, but of imagination—a failure to probe and speculate, to ask perceptive questions of the data. And, as we shall argue below, the failure to probe and speculate was a failure not of the shipping specialists but of the Sovietologist estimators.

Even more important, the information about the large-hatch ships was nothing more than suggestive. No action could have been taken on the basis of this kind of "soft" information, so alerting the top people would have served only to make them more sensitive to the possibility of missiles in Cuba. But it would have made little difference, since, as already described, the top officials were already so sensitive about the possibility of missiles in Cuba that they were quivering.

It has also been suggested that policy somehow inhibited the intelligence agencies. But there is no evidence of any attempt by the policy makers to suppress information or to hamper intelligence-gathering activities, except for Dean Rusk's suggestion that the U–2 make peripheral flights around Cuba and only for special reasons actually "dip into" Cuban airspace. But his motive was mainly to avoid a diplomatic brouhaha that might prevent any further U–2 flights, as happened after Gary Powers was shot down. No request from the intelligence community to fly a U–2 over Cuba was ever refused.

Also, the policy makers were equally alert to the possibility that the Soviets might put missiles in Cuba even though the September estimate concluded they would not. President Kennedy was worried about leaks if intelligence ever did come in on offensive weapons. He also wanted to ensure that if we were faced with missiles in Cuba there would be time to devise a policy for dealing with the problem before there was a public uproar. So, as already mentioned, in September he ordered a special security arrangement, Psalm, that ensured that everyone who would need to know would get intelligence on offensive weapons, but that no one else would get it. Such extraordinary measures would hardly have been taken if the policy makers were complacently confident that the Soviets would stop short of introducing missiles into Cuba.

Afterward there were only two attempts by insiders to allege that the policy makers interfered with intelligence, and both petered out. In the immediate wake of the crisis, everyone in the intelligence community was understandably nervous that an unfair case might be made against them by the Senate investigating committee. Reflecting this nervousness, John McCone in testifying before the committee seemed to suggest that George Ball's public testimony on October 3 was his own personal view and to imply that Ball's confident assurances did not represent the intelligence community's view and particularly not McCone's own personal view.

In those days, an uncorrected transcript of such testimony was sent not only to the person testifying, but also to the heads of the other intelligence agencies. After reading what McCone had said, I telephoned him and read him my memorandum for the record written after I had asked him to clear the statement that we had prepared for Ball. McCone readily acknowledged his mistake and struck that part of his testimony from the record.

The second incident was a study that McCone had instituted immediately after the crisis to determine if the missiles would have been discovered sooner if the secretary of state had not suggested substituting peripheral and "dipping" flights rather than the usual flights up one side of Cuba and down the other. For a while there was some uneasiness at the possibility that some real alley fighting might develop. But it was not difficult to show, first, that any delay caused by making four flights instead of one was negligible; second, that the risk of a U-2 being lost and an international crisis that would make it difficult to continue having any U-2 flights at all was real; and, third, that there had never been a turndown of any flight that the intelligence community had proposed, but that on the contrary both the White House and the State Department had actually pushed for more intelligence all along. In such circumstances, the study was conveniently forgotten, all the more easily as it became increasingly clear that the investigating committee was not going to make any sweeping accusations that the CIA and the intelligence community had failed.

After the crisis, the September 19 National Intelligence Estimate came in for heavy criticism from both inside and outside the intelligence community. The argument was that it did not pay enough attention to indications like the large-hatch ships, the braggings of Castro's pilot, the report of the long-trailer convoy, and the other subtle indications that seem significant in hindsight. But the information about the large-hatch ships and most of the refugee reports about long-trailer convoys was never put before the estimators, as we have seen, and all the rest of the reports came in *after* the September estimate was made. In addition, the estimate did warn that the military advantages of a successful deployment of missiles to Cuba would be sufficiently great that the intelligence community should be particularly alert.

The estimate reached the conclusion it did not just because putting missiles in Cuba would be inconsistent with past Soviet behavior. A more persuasive reason was that given the high risk of the missiles being discovered and the high probability of a strong American response, it would not be in the Soviet interest to put the missiles in Cuba. After all, intelligence estimators must assume that the other side is acting in its own best interest or their job is completely hopeless. And certainly in this respect—the consequences of putting missiles in Cuba for the Soviets' best interest—it was the American intelligence people who were right in their estimate and the Soviet policy makers who were wrong in theirs. In this sense, as Joseph Neubert, a Sovietologist in the State Department's intelligence bureau, remarked after the crisis was over, the only way the American analysts could have predicted Soviet behavior correctly would have been to estimate that the Soviets would mis-estimate!

There is another, more subtle point that should be made in defense of the September 19 estimate. When intelligence analysts predict without qualification that the other side *will* take a belligerent action, they force a policy decision. In effect, they preempt the policy makers. They *cannot* make this kind of estimate, and they will *never* make this kind of estimate unless the evidence is totally overwhelming and conclusive. But rarely in the affairs of humankind is the evidence totally overwhelming and conclusive.

Policy makers can and must make decisions on the basis of partial and inconclusive evidence. It is their job. To make such decisions, they must consider all the other threats to the nation and all the nation's other commitments. They must consider not only the probabilities of an estimate that the other side will take a certain action, but also the costs and probable effectiveness of the alternative ways of meeting the predicted threat or problem. The intelligence community does not have the information to make judgments on alternative policies and cannot cast their analysis in terms of such alternatives.

A vivid illustration of the differences between the tasks of the policy maker and those of intelligence officials who are responsible for estimating is contained in Churchill's war memoirs.[5]

Churchill writes that in the early months of 1941 British agents had reported extensive German troop movements to the Balkans, but that information on the movement to what was to be the main Russian front after the attack on June 22, 1941, was more difficult to obtain. At the same time a number of factors, such as continued German air attacks on Britain, the evidence of war supplies being sent from the Soviet Union to Germany, and the obvious interest both countries had in dividing up the British Empire, all combined to make everyone believe that Hitler and Stalin would make an agreement. Accordingly, the British Joint Intelligence Committee (JIC) rejected rumors current in Europe in early April of a German plan to attack the Soviet Union, and as late as May 23 they reported that the rumors had died down. It was not until June 5 that the JIC decided that there was a real possibility of a German attack on Russia, and not until June 12—only ten days before the attack began— that they felt they had enough evidence to say that Hitler had finally made up his mind.

Churchill, however, made his decision in *March*—a month before the intelligence community even considered the problem! He writes, with a touch of sarcasm, that he had never been content with the form of collective wisdom represented by the JIC, and that as early as 1940 he had arranged to see the agents' raw reports before they were sifted and digested by the various intelligence authorities. Thus, in March, 1941, Churchill saw an agent's report that three of the five panzer divisions moving toward Greece and Yugoslavia had been rerouted to Poland just after the agreement with Prince Paul of Yugoslavia and then sent quickly back to the Balkans again when Yugoslavia rebelled. This report, Churchill says, was for him "a lightning flash that illuminated the whole Eastern scene." It convinced Churchill that Hitler had planned to invade Russia in May and that the Belgrade revolt meant a delay until June. Accordingly, Churchill immediately sent a warning cable to Stalin.

In relating this story, Churchill implies that the JIC were simply stupid. But suggesting that the JIC should have predicted the German invasion on the basis of the movement of the panzer divisions is just as unfair as saying that the September 19 estimate should have predicted that the Soviets would send nuclear missiles to Cuba. Policy makers make predictions in terms of the probable costs and gains of accepting a prediction as a basis for action. But the JIC were charged simply with estimating probable developments. The JIC had neither the information about British goals, plans, and policies that was needed to assess the consequences of telling Stalin something that might not have come to pass, which might well have been serious, nor the right to make that kind of analysis. So the JIC was not free to force a decision until it had absolutely conclusive evidence.

Churchill, however, having both the information needed for a policy analysis and the responsibility for making that analysis, was in a position to evaluate the consequences of action on a prediction based on such partial evidence. Thus he could make a rational decision to go ahead, having determined that, even if the prediction turned out to have been wrong, the consequences of acting as if it were correct, or even of just waiting to see, would not be that bad. The consequences would be outweighed by the gains if the prediction turned out indeed to have been correct.

In the case of Cuba, most of the reports that seem so significant in hindsight—large-hatch ships riding high in the water, the braggings of Castro's pilot, and so on—did not provide any information that could have been the basis for further action, either targeting a U–2 or taking policy action. All that these reports could do, no matter how seriously they were taken, was to increase sensitivity in Washington to the possibility that the Soviets would put missiles in Cuba. But the people in Washington, as even the public statements of the time show, were, to repeat, sensitive to the point of paranoia. President Kennedy made several public statements warning the Soviets. He instituted the Psalm special clearance. Questions were asked on the subject in every congressional hearing that had even the remotest connection with Cuba. And everyone in official Washington talked about the possibility constantly.

The factors influencing the decision at the October 4 meeting to fly again over western Cuba were: (1) the need to check on how advanced the antiaircraft SAMs were in that part of Cuba, (2) the fact that there was an inland area that had not been covered since September 5, (3) the report of "unusual activity probably connected with missiles" in Pinar del Río, and (4) the two reports of long-trailer convoys heading west. The report of "unusual activity" was distributed the day before the meeting, on October 3, and the second report of a long-trailer convoy was distributed the very morning of the meeting, on October 4. So the only report containing information on which earlier action by the intelligence community could be based was the first report of a long-trailer convoy ("heading west"), which arrived in Washington on September 21.

For many years, it seemed to me that the way this report was handled was the only thing that could fairly be called a failure of the intelligence-gathering effort. I thought that CIA headquarters should have refrained from adding the comment that the agent had probably seen a 30-foot SAM trailer rather than a 60-foot MRBM trailer without some concrete evidence. I thought the intelligence community should have given more emphasis to this report and turned their attention to the western end of the island some 10 days to two weeks sooner than it did.

For years I believed that the agent had indeed seen a trailer 60 feet long carrying an MRBM and not a trailer 30 feet long carrying a SAM. For years I was critical of the CIA for having added what I thought was a gratuitous comment. Then years later I discovered that a CIA postmortem of the crisis—about which the CIA did not bother to tell me and several other people involved—concluded that the first visit of a large-hatch ship, the *Poltava,* was not until September 15. So what the agent saw was undoubtedly a trailer carrying a 30-foot-long SAM after all!

The CIA comment, however, did not make anyone in the government less sensitive to the possibility that the Soviets might put missiles in Cuba, although, combined with the overall judgment in the September 19 estimate that they would probably not do so, it undoubtedly led the people concerned to be more cautious about taking risks with the U–2 than they might otherwise have been. All through late September and early October, there was a determination to move slowly and deliberately. What was worrying both the intelligence and the policy people in Washington was the advancing state of readiness of the antiaircraft SAMs and the fact that these SAMs were more advanced models than we had seen before. In May, 1960, to repeat, Gary Powers' U–2 was shot down over the Soviet Union in circumstances that suggested that new SAMs had been developed that were effective at the U–2's top altitude. But the evidence was not conclusive. On September 10, 1962, again to repeat, right in the middle of the crisis, a Chinese Nationalist U–2 was shot down over Communist China. It then seemed perfectly obvious that if we were not exceptionally careful a U–2 might be shot down over Cuba. No one wanted to risk a pilot's life unnecessarily, and there was also another consideration. If a U–2 were shot down, there would be a political storm in the UN and all over the world of sizable proportions, as was so vividly illustrated when Powers' U–2 was shot down and the summit conference of 1960 wrecked. But it was not the certain political storm that caused the worry, but the real possibility that the fuss might work to deny us any further use of the U–2. Without the U–2, intelligence was blind.

The caution was entirely justified, but there might have been a greater sense of urgency if the overall judgment had been that the Soviets probably *would* put missiles in Cuba rather than that they probably would not.

But even so, as a practical matter, the difference at most would probably have been no more than a very few days. If the first of the MRBMs arrived in the port on September 15 and the convoy left on September 16 or 17, the soonest that the construction could have been recognized as missile sites was probably September 18, and the decision to look again at the western end of the island was actually made on October 4. Given the vagaries of the weather, it would have been a fantastic stroke of luck if convincing photographs could have been obtained before September 20 or 21—and convincing photographs were essential to win support for the kind of action that would be necessary.

Given the inherent difficulties of espionage and the special circumstances, the laboriousness and risk in recruiting agents, the time lag in communicating secretly with an agent once recruited, the risk of a U–2 being shot down and the possible restrictions this might impose on our best source of information, the frustration of cloud cover, the elaborate security precautions taken by the Soviets, and their efforts at deception—given all these difficulties it is something to be proud about that the missiles were discovered as early as they were. In sum, Cuba in 1962, it seems to me, must be marked down as a victory for the American intelligence community—and a victory of a very high order.

The major criticism that can be made of the intelligence-gathering effort is that as the scientific instruments of information gathering became so marvelous, the intelligence community, sharing the normal American love of technical gadgetry, had neglected the time-consuming and tedious methods of classical espionage. Recruiting, training, and putting an agent in place may take years, and it may be still more years before he or she reports anything of any significance. It is so much easier to send a U–2 or use some other scientific gadget. But there are some matters on which we need information that a U–2 camera cannot pick up. If there had been in Cuba a better network of traditional espionage agents, for example, the U–2 could have been dispatched sooner, guided more directly to suspected sites, and routed on a safer track.

On the other hand, the point must be immediately and emphatically made that traditional espionage—in the form of a spy in Moscow—did in fact make the photointerpreters more effective than they would otherwise have been. The spy, Oleg Penkovsky, was run jointly by the CIA and British intelligence under the code names *Ironbark* and *Chickadee*. He was a colonel in the GRU (military intelligence directorate) on assignment to the Government Committee on Science and Technology, and his job required him to make occasional trips abroad. On one such trip, he tried to defect to the West, but was persuaded to become what the intelligence community calls a "defector-in-place."

Penkovsky did not have access to information on high-level decisions such as the one to put missiles in Cuba. But he did succeed in smuggling out of the Soviet Union the manual used by the Soviet missile troops when they deployed an MRBM or an IRBM. Although the photointerpreters had gotten much of the background they needed to recognize the missile sites from studying U–2 and satellite photos of such sites being constructed in the Soviet Union, this manual undoubtedly made their task much easier.[6]

CONCLUSION: OVERALL SUCCESS AND ONE MAJOR FAILURE

But the most important fact in the whole intelligence-gathering story is that the missiles were discovered before they were operational—and long enough before to permit the U.S. government to assess the situation, develop a policy, and launch a course of action by the time the MRBMs did become operational and before the IRBMs even arrived.

Even if the 2,000-mile IRBMs had actually gotten to Cuba none would have been ready to launch until mid-November. On October 14, when the missiles were first discovered, the Soviets in an emergency could have launched at most one or two missiles from no more than two or three of the 1,000-mile MRBM sites for a maximum of six missiles. By October 28, when Khrushchev agreed to withdraw, the Soviets might have been able to fire an initial salvo of between 12 and 18 MRBMs. But by that time the American Strategic Air Command, Polaris submarines, and ICBM forces were on full alert, ready to go—and so was an invasion force.

In the end, the Soviets were caught, as then Senator Hubert H. Humphrey said, "with their rockets down and their missiles showing"—and caught in time.

THE ONE BIG FAILURE

In the above discussion the reader will have noticed that the judgment was that what was so marvelously successful was the "intelligence-gathering" effort. At one crucial point, the same cannot be said of the intelligence-*estimating* effort. Indeed, it can be persuasively argued that if the intelligence-estimating effort had been of a higher quality, the Soviets would have been dissuaded from ever putting the missiles in Cuba at all.

As already related, the intelligence community was opposed to telling the Soviets in the fall of 1961 that the United States had finally discovered that the missile gap was in favor of the United States and not the Soviet Union. The decision, to repeat, went against the intelligence community, and the Soviets were told through Gilpatric's speech and by briefing the members of NATO. Everyone—in the intelligence community, the State Department, and the White House—fully recognized that the Soviets would be alarmed and that they would feel it absolutely essential that they take effective countermeasures. What everyone expected was that the Soviets would launch a crash ICBM program to close the gap. But no one thought of the possibility that the Soviets would send missiles to Cuba.

The policy makers in the backs of their minds undoubtedly remembered that the Soviets had a surplus of MRBMs and IRBMs. But they could not be expected to make the necessary connections. That responsibility belonged to the intelligence community. It was the intelligence community that was responsible for dealing with the facts of the Soviet MRBM and IRBM capability every day, day in and day out. The single most important failure of the entire American effort in dealing with the Cuban missile crisis was the failure to recognize that putting missiles in Cuba was a cheap, if only temporary, solution to what everyone recognized the Soviets would regard as a very serious problem. As the director of the State Department's Bureau of Intelligence and Research at the time, I was as much to blame for this failure as anyone else.

If the intelligence community had recognized this possibility and brought it forcefully to the attention of the State Department, the White House, and the president, it is very probable that public warnings by the president would have persuaded the Soviets that an attempt to put missiles in Cuba would be a disaster and that there would therefore have been no missile crisis at all.

President Kennedy made his several efforts, public and private, to warn the Soviets that the United States would not tolerate their putting missiles in Cuba only in *September*—several weeks after the huge arms shipment was well under way.

Once Khrushchev and the leadership of the Soviet Union had made the decision to send missiles to Cuba and obtained Castro's permission, assembled the various weapons, loaded the ships, and started them on their way—once all these things had been done—it would have been difficult to the point of a practical political impossibility for them to reverse the decision. It would have been especially difficult to reverse the decision in the face of mere words—to reverse the decision just because the president of the United States had made some speeches and issued some private warnings.

Suppose, however, that the intelligence community had thought about what alternatives were open to the Soviets and had decided that putting missiles in Cuba was a real possibility. Suppose the intelligence community had forcefully presented this view to the policy makers. Suppose that Kennedy's warnings had therefore been issued and reissued beginning, say, in January of 1962, which would have been long enough after the Gilpatric speech and the NATO briefings that the Soviets would not interpret them as a preliminary to some sort of aggressive move against Berlin, Eastern Europe, or some other part of what the Soviets regarded as their own domain. Suppose the warnings had been repeated on suitable occasions both in public and in private throughout the spring. If so, it seems very probable that when Khrushchev was pacing up and down his hotel room in Bulgaria, his conclusion would have been that the worst way to try to solve the problem of the "missile gap in reverse" would be to send MRBMs and IRBMs to Cuba. If the American intelligence estimators had done their job with more imagination, in sum, there may never have been a Cuban missile crisis.

The failure to warn the Soviets of the consequences of putting missiles in Cuba, then, was the really big intelligence failure. Why did we fail? McGeorge Bundy put his finger on the reason when he said later that it "never occurred to us" to issue a warning earlier, and even when it was issued by Kennedy's speech in September, "We did it because of the requirements of domestic politics, not because we seriously believed that the Soviets would do anything as crazy from our standpoint as the placement of Soviet nuclear weapons in Cuba."

NOTES

1. Arthur M. Schlesinger, Jr., *A Thousand Days: John F. Kennedy in the White House* (Boston: Houghton-Mifflin, 1965), p. 821.

2. For an assessment of espionage, see my *Strategic Intelligence and National Decisions* (Glencoe, IL: The Free Press, 1956; reprinted 1982 by Greenwood Press, Westport, CT).

3. Since the second report arrived in Washington only the day before the October 4 meeting that decided to send the U–2 to cover the western end of the island, there is no reason to believe that it would have caused a decision to be made any sooner.

4. Roberta Wohlstetter, "Cuba and Pearl Harbor: Hindsight and Foresight," *Foreign Affairs* (July, 1965), p. 700.

5. Winston S. Churchill, *The Second World War,* vol. III, *The Grand Alliance* (Boston: Houghton-Mifflin, 1950), pp. 354–61. What follows was drawn from my *Strategic Intelligence and National Decisions* (Glencoe, IL: The Free Press, 1956) pp. 172–74.

6. Penkovsky was uncovered by Soviet counterespionage in the midst of the Cuban crisis, although not through any fault of the West. He was promptly tried and executed.

Chapter 4

The Initial American Reaction

It was late Monday afternoon, October 15, when the photographic interpreters found the first evidence of missiles on a U–2 picture of the San Cristóbal area in western Cuba. John McCone, the director of the CIA, had been called out of town in the middle of the afternoon that same day—his stepson had been killed in an accident in California—and it was Lieutenant General Marshall S. Carter and Ray S. Cline, both deputy directors of the CIA, who were the first to be informed. They each began to telephone to alert the government.

Carter called Lieutenant General Joseph F. Carroll, director of the Defense Intelligence Agency, who in turn called Roswell Gilpatric, deputy secretary of defense (Secretary McNamara was host that night for the "Hickory Hill University," an intellectual discussion group sponsored by Robert Kennedy, and was not told until about midnight). Carroll, with two intelligence experts, then went to see General Maxwell D. Taylor, newly appointed chairman of the Joint Chiefs of Staff, who was giving a dinner party at his home. There in a back room certain of the guests were briefed—Taylor, Gilpatric, and U. Alexis Johnson, deputy under secretary of state for political affairs.

As Carter was alerting the Defense Department, Cline was calling McGeorge Bundy, the president's national security adviser, and then me, who was director of intelligence and research at the State Department.

Cline reached Bundy at home. After making sure that all the necessary wheels were in motion, Bundy decided not to disturb the president that night. He was going to need all the rest he could get. "At that point," Bundy later explained, "the President could only have fretted; and it seemed best to give the staff a chance to get rolling and get the intelligence materials in order, for the central requirement at that time was not haste, but the development of an effective plan of action."

The next morning—just before 9 a.m.—Bundy briefed the president in his bedroom. The president, still in his bathrobe, instructed Bundy to arrange for a meeting at 11:45 that morning of what became known as the ExCom, the Executive Committee of the National Security Council.

Cline reached me on my White House phone about 9 p.m. Monday evening. The White House phone was a secure, scrambler phone, which permitted uninhibited top secret conversations. But Cline was cryptic—even obtuse and evasive. I thought he must be ill. Later, I discovered that he thought that because I was so slow to understand what he was trying to tell me, I must have had one drink too many at dinner. Thirty years later we finally got a chance to compare notes. He was being cryptic because he was talking from a pay phone, and he did not realize that I thought that he, too, was on a secure White House phone.

I immediately started trying to reach the secretary of state. He was hosting a dinner for Gerhard Schroeder, the German foreign minister, in one of the formal dining rooms on the top floor of the State Department, and getting him to the phone without arousing suspicion took some doing.

I finally reached the security officer accompanying the secretary, and he managed to have Rusk passed a note to call me at home—urgently. At the first opportunity, Rusk excused himself for a moment and slipped out to use the phone in the pantry.

When he explained that he was not using a secure phone, I "double-talked" the news. "Do you remember the conversation about possible developments down south that we had in your office last week?" He said that he did. "Well," I said, "they are there."

"Do you think this is it?" Rusk asked.

"There has been time for only a preliminary analysis," I replied, "but from what I can get over the phone there doesn't seem to be any doubt."

Rusk asked me to meet him in his office first thing the next morning, and I continued with my phoning. George W. Ball, the under secretary, and the assistant secretaries for European and Latin American affairs both had to be informed. I also had to get our own experts in the Bureau of Intelligence and Research started to work. I was able to reach everyone on the secure phone except Edwin M. Martin, the assistant secretary for Latin American affairs.

Martin was at the National Press Club giving a speech, the main theme of which, ironically, was that the military buildup in Cuba was, according to the evidence, "basically defensive in character." I reached one of his aides on the phone, who explained that Martin was still on the platform and asked whether the matter was urgent enough to interrupt. "For God's sake, no!" I said. "But have him call me when he's finished—but don't attract attention." Martin called from a pay phone, ostensibly to tell his wife he was on his way home, and again I "double-talked" the news.

THE EXCOM MEETING

What was to become the ExCom met the next morning, on Tuesday, October 16, in the Cabinet room in the low-lying west wing of the White House, and the president decided immediately to put Cuba under virtually continuous air surveillance. From that time on, there was hardly an hour of daylight that did not see a U–2 over some part of Cuba.

After that decision, the first item on the agenda was the question "Why?" What did the Soviets intend to do with these missiles they were so massively deploying to Cuba, just 90 miles from the American coast?[1]

In the discussion that followed almost all the major issues that had to be faced in the succeeding days were touched upon. What had motivated the Soviets in their decision to put missiles in Cuba? What did they hope to accomplish? Were the missiles in Cuba designed as an umbrella for a Soviet seizure of Berlin? Was this a sober decision, or an impetuous act similar to the time Khrushchev took off one of his shoes at a UN meeting and pounded on the desk in front of him to express his anger? Was it Khrushchev's decision? Or did it mean that Khrushchev and his policy of peaceful coexistence were being superseded by a military takeover of the Kremlin? Were the missiles in Cuba only the preliminary to an attack on the United States itself?

Another issue was what this sudden jump in the nuclear mega-tonnage the Soviets could deliver on the American heartland would portend for the balance of power in the world. Secretary of Defense Robert McNamara initially and for two or three days thereafter argued that Soviet missiles in Cuba made no real difference. Soviet ICBMs could already reach the United States, and the Soviets would undoubtedly continue to build ICBMs no matter what happened in Cuba. His conclusion was that putting medium- and intermediate-range missiles in Cuba merely permitted the Soviets to begin to close the gap in 1962 rather than a few years later. "A missile is a missile," was McNamara's argument. "It makes no great difference whether you are killed by a missile fired from the Soviet Union or from Cuba." The clear implication of McNamara's position was that the United States should do nothing, but simply accept the presence of Soviet missiles in Cuba and sit tight.

But several of the others disagreed, arguing that while the military consequences might not be overwhelming, they were certainly significant—and the political consequences were very serious indeed. Such a sudden shift in the strategic balance, the others felt, would give the Soviets untold political opportunities even if they did not intend to use the missiles in a purely military sense. And the political consequences of a sudden and dramatic closing of the gap were fundamentally different from a gradual evening out over a period of years.

Paul Nitze, then assistant secretary of defense for international security affairs, disagreed with McNamara on the military issue as well as on the political. The manned bomber force of the Strategic Air Command was based largely in the southern part of the United States, and it would be very vulnerable to missiles in Cuba. Missiles fired from the Soviet Union could be detected soon enough to provide 15 minutes' warning, but missiles fired from Cuba would permit a warning of only two or three minutes.

A third issue was what the American objective should be. Should our purpose be limited to getting the offensive weapons out of Cuba? Or should we set a larger goal—removing the Soviet presence entirely and eliminating Castro and his regime?

A final issue was how this objective was to be accomplished. Realistically, what were the alternative courses of action open to the United States, and how effective would each alternative be?

There were four major kinds of action the United States might take, each with several variants.

One was simply to do nothing. As mentioned above, it was toward this alternative that McNamara's initial assessment pointed. If the missiles in Cuba made no real difference to the strategic balance and the world political stability resting on that balance, there would be no sense in running the risk of getting them out.

A second alternative was political and diplomatic action—to protest to Khrushchev, to go to the UN, to enlist the support of the Organization of American States, and so on.

A third alternative was to take out the missiles in a quick military move, with or without advance warning. Selective air strikes could be used to destroy the missile installations; parachute troops could be used to seize them in a *coup de main;* or the United States could launch a full-scale invasion of Cuba if the Soviets did not reverse their course.

DOMESTIC POLITICAL PRESSURES

There was one special but peculiarly significant set of pressures bearing on the policy choices before the group that was not discussed at all in the ExCom meetings—although its presence must certainly have been felt. Behind the policy choices loomed domestic politics and an appalling array of rival interests and competing factions—beginning with those who had all along wanted nothing better than an invasion of Cuba, even at the risk of war and the cost to other American objectives.

The fact of the matter was that President Kennedy and his administration were peculiarly vulnerable on Cuba. He had used it in his campaign against Nixon to great effect, asking over and over why a Communist regime had been permitted to come to power just 90 miles off our coast. Then came the Bay of Pigs, and now the Soviets were turning Cuba into an offensive military base.

Senator Keating, Senator Goldwater, and others had attacked the administration's policy toward Cuba and the Soviet program of arms aid as a "do-nothing" policy, as we have seen. These political pressures—and the administration's response to them—had already foreclosed some of the policy alternatives. The administration had not been able to say publicly that it was flying U–2s over Cuba and that it was therefore absolutely certain that its information on the weapons in Cuba up to that moment was accurate. Indeed, there was some risk of exposing our sources in merely acting confident about the accuracy of official information. Thus in trying to meet the opposition's charges and to reassure the public without actually saying why it was so confident, the administration fell into the semantic trap of trying to distinguish between "offensive" and "defensive" weapons.

In addition, Keating, Goldwater, and the others had beaten the drums so loudly that Kennedy had been forced not only to deny that "offensive" weapons were in Cuba but to put himself on the public record that his administration would not tolerate their being put there in the future.

At the time that Kennedy made those statements, he knew from incontrovertible evidence that there were no long-range missiles in Cuba, and he had the assurances of specialists on the Soviet Union that the Kremlin leaders were not likely to put them there in the future. Thus at the time the statements were made, they seemed to be a necessary political response to the opposition charges. Second, they seemed to contain little risk of being proved wrong—if the Soviet experts knew their business as well as they had many times demonstrated that they did. And, finally, Kennedy's statements seemed to be a useful warning to the Soviets that would reinforce their natural caution.

On the other hand, if the missiles were not important enough strategically to justify a confrontation with the Soviet Union, as McNamara originally thought, yet were "offensive," the administration would be damned if it failed to take action but it would be equally damned if it took unnecessary and risky action. And the greatest illusion of all would be for anyone to think that the Capitol Hill advocates of a more belligerent policy would support the president if it turned out that a belligerent policy was not appropriate. No one could forget that Senator Robert A. Taft, leader of the Republican opposition during the Korean War, had praised President Truman's decision to fight in Korea in the 24 hours after it was made, but within a few short weeks had begun to call it "Truman's War."

However, as the buildup proceeded it became increasingly clear that McNamara's original reaction was very, very wrong. In the first place, the missiles that the Soviet Union was deploying to Cuba would *double* the number of nuclear warheads that the Soviet Union could deliver on targets in the United States. Even worse, once the missiles were in place and secure behind a protective antiaircraft and ground defense shield there would be nothing at all to prevent the Soviets from steadily increasing the number until they had enough to fire two, three, or more missiles at every city and military target in the United States with the sole exception of Seattle.

But since no one shared McNamara's view that the missiles were not important strategically and since even he came to change it, the more important issue was at the other end of the spectrum. Not only had the political give-and-take led the administration into the "offensive" versus "defensive" dichotomy, but in responding to the charges that Kennedy was following a "do-nothing" policy, administration spokesmen had come dangerously close to ruling out one major alternative by several times saying—correctly by any normal reading of international law—that a blockade of Cuba would be an "act of war."

What President Kennedy also had to remember was that not all of the opposition was outside the administration and the executive branch. The aphorism coined by Charles G. Dawes, Coolidge's vice president, that the members of the Cabinet were a president's "natural enemies" was as relevant now as it had been throughout history. Applied to the members of the ExCom in these particular circumstances, Dawes' aphorism was an exaggeration; applied more widely in the government, it was not.

Already some mild attempts had been made to push a more belligerent point of view by leaking slightly distorted information. Before George Ball had begun his congressional testimony on October 3 about the then current status of Soviet arms in Cuba, for example, all the information in Ball's statement had already been leaked to the members of the committee and embellished to give the shore-to-ship harbor defense missiles Ball described a longer range than the 35 to 40 miles the intelligence experts assigned to them. "Information has come to my hand . . . ," said the chairman, Representative Paul Kitchin, "that Cuba has received in recent days some air-breathing type offensive missiles with a range, with a booster effort, of some 130 nautical miles. If that is true, I would certainly think that would be an offensive weapon." The briefers explained that it was true that with a booster that particular missile would have a range of 130 miles, but once past the controlling radar's range of 40 miles the missile was just as likely to hit Havana as Florida. This particular incident was unimportant; but it was a harbinger of much worse that was very likely to come, and soon.

There was, of course, not really any viciousness in the motives behind these seemingly disloyal efforts within the executive branch to block the administration from adopting one policy and forcing it to adopt another. Such efforts were only the normal and expected manifestation of the politics of policy making. In every department of the government there were men and women with deep and passionate convictions on policy. One of President Kennedy's major problems in the Cuban missile crisis—as with all presidents facing crises—was to free himself sufficiently from these political pressures, outside and inside the government, so that he could deal effectively with the Soviets and Cuba.

THE NEED FOR SECRECY

None of this was discussed at the first meeting of the ExCom on October 16, to repeat, although much of it must have been felt. But before the meeting broke up, the president did make one more decision—that we must avoid giving the Soviets any opportunity to grab the initiative. The risk that Soviet radar would spot a U–2 had to be taken, but there should be no public disclosure of the fact that we knew of the Soviet missiles in Cuba until a course of action had been decided upon and readied. If at all possible the two announcements—what the United States had discovered about Soviet missiles in Cuba and what the United States intended to do about it—should be made simultaneously. Security was therefore essential, and the president made it clear that he was determined that for once in the history of Washington there would be no leaks whatsoever.

The decision to couple disclosure with an announcement of the U.S. response was not so inconsequential as it sounded—it expressed the president's determination not to be dragged along in the wake of events, but to control them.

It was also not so easy to carry out. Leaks are hard to stop—mainly because of their usefulness to "inside opposition" as an instrument to block one policy or further another. But leaks are also hard to stop because of the normal human desire to look important, to impress friends and the press, to make people understand that one is really a part of the inner circle, privy to all sorts of vital state secrets. And probably no state secret of the whole century had been so vital as this one. Thus the decision to couple disclosure with an announcement of the American response imposed a very tight deadline on analysis, on decision, and on the preparations to implement the decision.

THE AMERICAN COVER AND DECEPTION

One other consequence of the decision to delay disclosure was that the United States also needed a program of cover and deception of its own. Life in Washington had to look normal over the next few days; and, by and large, it did. Between ExCom meetings the president sandwiched routine activities. On the morning of October 16, he kept a date with astronaut Walter N. Schirra, Mrs. Schirra, and their two children and showed them his daughter Caroline's pony while the ExCom was assembling in the Cabinet room. On Wednesday, October 17, he flew to Connecticut to keep some campaign speaking engagements. On Thursday, he presented some awards; met on domestic issues with the Cabinet; received a foreign visitor, Eisaku Sato, former finance minister of Japan; and, finally, had a long session with the visiting Soviet foreign minister, Andrei A. Gromyko.

Although the Soviets may have designed this grotesque meeting to serve their own purposes of cover and deception, it may have worked out to serve the American attempt at cover and deception even better. Gromyko began by warning President Kennedy that the Soviets were becoming impatient about Berlin and following the American elections would be compelled to sign a peace treaty with Communist East Germany. He then complained of the resolution passed by Congress, the measure authorizing the call-up of reserves, and so on. Finally, he read from his notes the statement that the Soviet arms aid to Cuba "was by no means offensive. If it were otherwise, the Soviet Government would have never become involved in rendering such assistance."

It was then that Kennedy repeated his warning of September 4 and 13, by actually reading Gromyko the texts. As suggested above, the effect may well have been to add another indication that the United States had probably learned about the missiles.

But if this is what happened, then the incident must also have reinforced the Soviet belief that the United States did not intend to do anything really drastic about the missiles—at least until after the elections—and so lulled the Soviets into a false sense of security.

On Friday, October 19, the president went to Cleveland and then on to Chicago to fill more commitments for campaign speeches. But the ExCom was now ready to make its recommendations for a decision. Robert Kennedy telephoned the president that he was needed in Washington. So on Saturday President Kennedy canceled the rest of the trip and returned to Washington—ostensibly because of an "upper respiratory infection" and a slight temperature. Even on the day of the denouement, October 22, Kennedy chatted on and on with Prime Minister Milton Obote of Uganda while the entire Cabinet waited.

The rest of the government also kept up the pretense of "business as usual." A long-scheduled amphibious exercise permitted the Navy to concentrate several dozen ships and 5,000 marines in the Caribbean without attracting undue attention. The Joint Chiefs of Staff were asked to remain in Washington for six weeks because of the urgencies of "budget planning." Everyone tried to keep up social engagements, although they sorely needed both the time and the rest that social engagements cost them. At one stage, to avoid attracting the attention that a whole fleet of long black cars going to the White House would have done, nine members of the ExCom piled into a single limousine, sitting on each other's laps, drove to the Treasury building, and made their way to the White House through an almost forgotten underground passage. A mock meeting was set up at the White House, ostentatiously attended by W. Averell Harriman, then assistant secretary of state for Far Eastern affairs, and Phillips Talbot, assistant secretary for Near Eastern and South Asian affairs.

Even so, there were some near misses. One afternoon someone looked out of a State Department window at the long line of black limousines drawn up at the diplomatic entrance, and thereafter high officials were driven into the basement and whisked upstairs in the secretary of state's private elevator. After Gromyko's meeting with the president, there was a dinner for him at the State Department.

Reporters saw McNamara and McCone arriving for a working session of the ExCom, which was held at the State Department in George Ball's conference room when the president was scheduled not to attend, and wondered what the secretary of defense and especially the director of central intelligence were doing at a dinner for Gromyko.

But without doubt the most important lucky break of all for the United States was the Soviet failure to realize that the U-2 was flying over Cuba almost constantly. If the Soviets had concluded that we knew about the missiles but deduced from the seeming lack of activity that we did not intend to do very much about them, the heavy traffic of the U-2s high in the Cuban sky would have been a dead giveaway. A U-2 at an altitude of 14 miles was beyond the vision of Cuban radar, but the radar the Soviets were putting in could easily pick it up. The only explanation seems to be that the new radar was not yet operational.

THE UNITED STATES INTELLIGENCE BOARD

The USIB met to analyze the daily reports from the U-2 flights at least twice daily—not at the glossy new CIA building in Langley, Virginia, which was their usual meeting place, but in one of the old OSS-CIA buildings in Foggy Bottom. Construction on all the missile sites was proceeding rapidly. Although the IRBMs were some distance from completion, the MRBMs would be ready much sooner. There was not much time.

As to the effect of the Soviets putting missiles in Cuba on the world balance of power, the intelligence community had no doubts. When both the MRBMs and the IRBMs were fully operational they could deliver an initial salvo of 40 missiles, each propelling a warhead of one megaton, as already described. The flight time to their targets could be measured in minutes. And unless the United States could get in a full retaliatory blow almost immediately and completely destroy the launching pads, this initial salvo could be followed by another within an hour or two, the time it took to reload.

Both the MRBMs and the IRBMs were above ground and "soft"—very vulnerable to attack—and therefore useful mainly in a first strike. In such a first strike, the MRBMs could reach and take out most of our manned bomber bases in the southern and south-western United States. The IRBMs could hit the ICBM bases in the northern parts of the United States, in such places as Wyoming and Montana, and, as already mentioned, once they were operational, the MRBMs and IRBMs between the two of them could reach every major city in the country except Seattle.

The intelligence community concluded that the deployment did not tip the balance so far that the Soviets would have an overall advantage in total megatons on target. However, by stationing these missiles in Cuba the Soviets had increased the destructive power they could deliver on target in the United States by over 50 percent. Worse, the increase in firepower would give the Soviets enough to erode the American capacity to strike back—and hence enough to degrade the ultimate deterrent. And once the system was in place and operational, the Soviets could send in still more missiles, until they had an overwhelming advantage, at least in a first strike.

NOTE

1. The records of the ExCom discussions are excellent, principally because the president took the precaution of having a tape recorder installed in the Cabinet room, which Mrs. Lincoln could turn on at a buzzer signal from Kennedy. Prior to this time, the only recording equipment in the Kennedy White House was in a drawer of Kennedy's desk in the Oval Office, which he could turn on himself when it was needed, although the quality was very poor.

Chapter 5

The Question of Soviet Motives

When the ExCom met the next day, on Wednesday, October 17, they returned to the question of Soviet motives. Did the Soviets intend to use the missiles for a surprise attack similar to the Japanese attack on Pearl Harbor? Or had the Soviets misinterpreted some piece of intelligence and therefore come to believe that the United States was about to attack them or their ally, Cuba? Or was the motive political, designed as an instrument for blackmailing the United States into, say, giving up Berlin?[1]

Determining the Soviet motive was crucial. If the Soviets intended to use the missiles to launch a surprise attack, the United States had no choice but to use force to remove them immediately. On the other hand, if the Soviets intended to use the missiles for some sort of political blackmail, the United States might find a way to deal with the situation without any actual shooting.

Various members of the ExCom came up with a total of six possible explanations. Four were rejected, and two were accepted.

1. Defense of Cuba: the first explanation considered was that the missiles were intended for the defense of Cuba. Perhaps the Soviets

and Castro feared that the United States would invade with American troops to make up for the failure of the Cuban brigade at the Bay of Pigs.

This explanation was rejected. Since President Kennedy had refused to use American forces to help the anti-Castro Cuban brigade at the Bay of Pigs, the Soviets would understand that he would hardly approve an American invasion at this time. Even if the Soviets did fear an American invasion, nuclear missiles were hardly necessary. Just a few Soviet troops would be a perfectly adequate deterrent. After all, one battalion each of American, British, and French forces had provided an adequate, plate-glass-window deterrent in Berlin for years. Why not the Soviet equivalent in Cuba?

2. A diverting trap: the second explanation considered was the notion of a diverting trap. Perhaps the Soviets thought that putting missiles in Cuba would actually provoke the United States into invading. If the giant United States actually did invade little Cuba, both its European Allies and American domestic opinion would be horrified. The Soviets could then take Berlin with impunity.

This explanation was also rejected. Using such a massive deployment for the sole purpose of a mere diversion would be much too costly. It would also be much too risky.

3. Trading Berlin for Cuba: the third explanation considered was Secretary of State Dean Rusk's variation of the "diverting trap" theory. Perhaps, Rusk suggested, the Soviets intended to get the missiles in place secretly. Then in a dramatic gesture at the UN the Soviets could pull back the curtain, reveal the missiles, and offer to trade Cuba for Berlin.

This explanation was also rejected, again on the grounds that it was both too costly and too risky. In addition, what would the rest of the Communist world think if Moscow sacrificed its Cuban ally so brutally and cynically?

4. Cuba missiles for Turkey missiles: the fourth explanation considered was the possibility that the Soviets wanted to exchange the missiles in Cuba for the American Jupiter missiles in Turkey.

This explanation was also rejected. The decision in the Eisenhower administration to send Jupiter missiles to Turkey and Italy and Thor missiles to the United Kingdom had been made at the request of the NATO Allies as a response to the Soviet deployment of MRBMs and IRBMs aimed at Europe in the western areas of the Soviet Union. The Jupiters were already obsolete when they were sent to Turkey.[2] They had a long countdown and were very vulnerable to a sniper on a hill a mile away. The purpose in deploying them had been largely symbolic, to demonstrate American nuclear support for the European Allies in the face of the Soviet deployment of IRBMs and MRBMs aimed solely at those Allies. The Soviets also knew that some months earlier Kennedy had ordered the Jupiters to be withdrawn as soon as Turkish agreement could be obtained. Since the Soviets knew all this, it was very doubtful that they would agree to a trade even if the United States offered one.[3]

5. The missile gap in reverse: the fifth explanation considered was the so-called missile gap in reverse.

To repeat, the decision to tell the Soviets that the United States had learned that the missile gap was actually in favor of the United States was made in full appreciation of the very high probability that the Soviets would take some sort of countermeasures. At the time, it was assumed that the main countermeasure would probably be a crash ICBM program. Now, a year later, it seemed logical to conclude that the Soviets were deploying their MRBMs and IRBMs, of which they had a vast oversupply, as a "quick fix" for what came to be called the missile gap in reverse.

This explanation was accepted. The Soviets certainly could not believe that the rather vulnerable MRBMs and IRBMs would be an effective substitute for hardened ICBMs. But the MRBMs and IRBMs would be a useful stopgap until the Soviet ICBM program got into full production and deployment.

However, some members of the ExCom found it puzzling that the Soviets thought they could succeed in deploying the missiles secretly when they must have known that the United States was flying U–2s over Cuba.

6. A Cold War probe: the final explanation offered was that the Soviet deployment of missiles to Cuba was a Cold War probe. Khrushchev had told the American poet Robert Frost when he visited Moscow that the West was "too liberal to fight." Kennedy was a new and inexperienced president with a very narrow electoral victory. The Soviets might have thought, "Why not test the will of the West and the will of the new president?" They could always pull back if the United States reacted strongly, the Soviets might have reasoned, and if the United States weakened over the missiles in Cuba, the Soviets could push their advantage in Berlin and even more in Latin America.

Ambassador Llewellyn Thompson, a lifetime specialist on the Soviet Union, pointed out that a favorite adage of the Soviet Communist leaders going all the way back to Lenin was that if an enemy left an opening you should thrust hard with your bayonet. If you met only soft flesh, you should push even harder. But if you met solid bone, you should then withdraw. So the explanation was also accepted that the Soviet Union had put the missiles in Cuba to test the will of the West and of the new, young president.

But even though these two explanations were accepted, some members of the ExCom had doubts and counterarguments. On the proposition that the missiles were sent to Cuba to redress the missile gap in reverse, the counterargument began with the point that even though the Soviet Union had a huge surplus of MRBMs and IRBMs, these missiles were "soft"; that is, they were not housed in silos of reinforced concrete. "Soft" missiles were vulnerable to attack by conventional weapons—even, as already mentioned, by a man with a rifle. The countdown time to launch MRBMs and IRBMs was rather long. For both these reasons the missiles the Soviets had deployed to Cuba were not really a substitute for large-warhead ICBMs based in the Soviet Union in well-protected, "hardened" silos. In strategic parlance, these latter missiles were "second-strike" weapons that were able to receive a nuclear blow and still strike back. The MRBMs and IRBMs were both too vulnerable and too slow in counting down to qualify as second-strike weapons.

In fact, the counterargument continued, the Soviet MRBMs and IRBMs did not even qualify as fully adequate first-strike weapons. A first-strike weapon is one that is capable of destroying the enemy's missiles and bombers before they can be launched. First-strike weapons must not only be fast in counting down but extremely accurate. The MRBMs and IRBMs were deficient in both qualities. However, the counterargument did concede that the MRBMs and IRBMs did have enough first-strike capability to be significant—partly because the American radar and defense system was designed mainly to detect an attack from the North rather than from the South. In the words of the official National Intelligence Estimate, the MRBMs and IRBMs would "begin to degrade the United States second-strike capability."

So the question before the ExCom became: if the Soviet MRBMs and IRBMs did not qualify as second-strike weapons and were not fully adequate as first-strike weapons, how could the Soviets believe that the MRBMs and IRBMs were a "quick fix"? The MRBMs and IRBMs could do the United States great damage, but in retaliation the United States could do the Soviet Union even greater damage. The United States could, in fact, utterly destroy it.

So the first motive, to redress the missile gap in reverse, seemed to be less than fully rational. However, the counterargument did concede that nations sometimes base rather fateful decisions at least in part on wishful thinking.

But the second motive, a Cold War probe of the will and determination of the United States and the new president, according to the counterargument, hardly stood up to close examination at all. The counterargument began with the point that the Soviets knew all about the capabilities of the U–2 reconnaissance plane. They had shot down Gary Powers and his U–2 in 1960, and they knew that it could take pictures with a remarkable resolution from an altitude of 14 miles. In logic, before the Soviets made the decision to deploy the missiles and went to Castro for permission, they must have assumed that the U–2 was flying regularly over Cuba.

Then when the Soviet arms buildup in Cuba actually began in the summer of 1962, President Kennedy and Secretary of State Rusk had instructed me, in my capacity as director of intelligence and research at the State Department, to give regular background briefings to the press describing in great detail what was unloaded from each Soviet freighter that docked in Cuba. The Soviets could not help but realize that such detailed information could only come from U–2 flights.

So unless the Soviets were guilty of a monumental oversight, they certainly ought to have realized that the United States would discover the missiles before they were fully operational. If they did realize that the United States would probably discover the missiles, the argument continued, it seems inconceivable that the Soviets would think that the United States would sit idly by and watch the missiles being deployed. In prudence the Soviets had to assume that the United States would react strongly. There would be a political and diplomatic crisis of formidable proportions, and the United States might well resort to military force—an air strike against the missiles, an invasion of Cuba, or even more drastic action.

In the light of all this and the extraordinary risk that deploying the missiles to Cuba would create, how could the Soviets possibly conclude that a Cold War probe in Cuba was worth it? Even as

President Kennedy accepted the notion that the Soviets might be engaging in a Cold War probe, he expressed some puzzlement. "If they doubted our guts" he said, "why didn't they just take Berlin? Why horse around with Cuba?"

Finally, the doubters concluded, the two explanations—a "quick fix" and a "Cold War probe"—were logically inconsistent. How could the Soviets justify embarking on an adventurous policy of probing the American will when at the very same time they perceived themselves at such a disadvantage in strategic missiles that they embarked on a risky deployment of their surplus MRBMs and IRBMs?

And they *were* at a strategic disadvantage. If matters came to a showdown, it would be the Soviets who would most likely be on the losing end. To "probe" the American will and determination in such circumstances would be madness. This was especially true because the Soviets, if the "quick-fix" argument holds, actually perceived themselves at a disadvantage.

Thus the Soviet motive, the doubters concluded, cannot really have been *both* a quick fix and a Cold War probe. If the motive was one or the other of the two, the quick fix was considerably more credible than the Cold War probe.

But to add to the puzzlement, the counterarguments against the "quick fix" are rather persuasive when one considers the alternative policy that the Soviets could have pursued. If they were concerned about their strategic imbalance, a more logical and considerably less risky policy would have been to do what they finally did do after they withdrew the missiles. When Kennedy offered an olive branch in his American University speech after the missile crisis, the Soviets accepted, eased off tensions, negotiated the limited nuclear test ban agreement, and cooperated with the Kennedy administration in bringing about what later became detente. Then, in the more relaxed climate that followed they built up their defenses over the next 15 years until they reached parity with the United States in not only strategic weapons but other types as well. A wiser response to the revelation that the United States had learned that the "missile gap" was actually in its favor would have been to do what they ultimately did do. There is no reason to believe that Kennedy would not have been as willing to consider detente before the Cuban missile crisis as he was after it.

THE DIFFERING MODES OF ANALYSIS

In concluding that the Soviet motives were, first, a "quick fix" of the "missile gap in reverse" and, second, a probe of the will of the West and of the new president, the members of the ExCom were implicitly assuming that the Soviet Union was acting as a monolith—that states have goals, that they examine alternatives for achieving those goals systematically, and that they choose between alternatives rationally, considering the relative costs and gains to the state of each alternative. The members of the ExCom, in a word, were using what has been variously called the classical, traditional, or "black box" mode of analysis—which, at least since the rise of the nation-state, is the way that most people have gone about answering questions about why states behaved the way they did.[4]

This approach assumes that the actors in international politics are states and that states have goals—principally to survive, to defend what they have, and to add to their power. As a result, in this kind of analysis strategic and geopolitical factors dominate.

As to the utility of this mode of analysis, as a noted scholar, Hans Morgenthau, once said, it "provides for rational discipline in action and creates that astounding continuity in foreign policy which makes American, British, or Russian foreign policy appear as an intelligible, rational continuum . . . regardless of the different motives, preferences, and intellectual and moral qualities of successive statesmen."

Using this strategic, geopolitical mode of analysis, the analyst doesn't need to know anything about the leaders of a state. It is assumed they will behave the same no matter who they are. The czar of Russia will behave the same as the secretary-general of the Communist Party of the Soviet Union. It doesn't really matter that one state was a monarchy and the other a Communist dictatorship, the argument goes; both behaved the same. Both sought a warm-water port, both tried to balance the powers of Europe, both tried to build a wall of buffer states between Russia and Europe. In the view of the strategic, geopolitical model, the personalities, abilities, and ideologies of the different leaders were all simply irrelevant.

Thus strategic analysts speak as often of China, the United States, and the Soviet Union as they do of Mao Zedong or Deng Xiaoping; of Stalin, Khrushchev, or Gorbachev; or of Roosevelt, Kennedy,

Reagan, Bush, or Clinton. Analysts talk in shorthand: "Moscow thinks this, Washington wants that, and Beijing is angry about something else." The actors in international politics are like black boxes. The analyst has no need to know what goes on inside the boxes. Some of the boxes are big, some small. Some have good economic resources to build military power, some poor. Some have good strategic locations, and some don't. And these things are all that the analyst needs to know about them.

A POLITICAL PROCESS MODE OF ANALYSIS

Another approach—called the "political process model" (or in a somewhat narrower variation, the "bureaucratic process model")—assumes that states are not monolithic but are made up of a variety of power centers. In the case of the Soviet Union, the most important of these power centers were the party bosses, the KGB, and the military. Others with little if any power on the larger questions but with some power on questions in the field of their particular responsibility were the top officials in the bureaucracies of the various economic enterprises and the officials of the party apparatus and local government in the different regions. (Khrushchev, for example, had his original power base in the Ukraine, where he was the party boss for years.)

Analysts using this approach assumed that policy in the Soviet Union on the big issues was made in a struggle among the three most powerful power centers—the party bosses, the KGB, and the military. They assumed that these power centers shared a commitment to state goals, but that they also had different organizational and personal goals.

In applying this model to the Cuban missile crisis, the hypothesis would be that the top people in these power centers supported the decision to put missiles in Cuba, or acquiesced in it, because they came to believe the move not only would serve the interests of the Soviet state but also would meet their own overall policy preferences in terms of ideology, philosophy, and expectations about the nature of international politics, would serve some parochial personal or organizational interest, or at the least would not harm their personal and parochial interests.

Second, analysts would then look for differences in goals or disagreements about means in regard to the particular issue. In the case of the decision to deploy missiles to Cuba, the American superiority in missiles and the fact that the Americans now knew they had superiority presented the Soviets with a problem. Outside analysts could safely assume that the Soviet military would argue for a crash ICBM program to close the missile gap as fast as possible. They could also safely assume that some of the top party and at least some of the KGB leaders would oppose a crash program and would argue for a stretched-out program to avoid disrupting the economy and growth in heavy industry.

However, as mentioned earlier, the Soviet Union had a huge oversupply of MRBMs and IRBMs, and at some point in the debate someone must have pointed to Castro's insistent appeals for arms for Cuba to defend itself against the United States and suggested deploying missiles to Cuba as a temporary solution to both the problem of the strategic imbalance and Castro's demands.

Using this analysis Western analysts could craft the following set of hypotheses about the various power centers.

First, the military would not be entirely happy with the compromise of sending MRBMs and IRBMs to Cuba, but this deployment would be at least half of the loaf they wanted. Deploying the missiles would partly redress the immediate imbalance until a buildup of ICBMs could take place.

For those top leaders concerned about the effect on the various economic enterprises, the compromise provided a real victory, since a stretched-out program would not greatly disturb the plans for long-term growth, as a crash ICBM program would do.

As for the rest of the party leaders, if deploying missiles to Cuba would placate both those who were concerned about the military problem and those concerned about the effects on the economy, they would obviously regard the deployment as a plus. Beyond that, deploying the missiles would score a victory against the United States that would be useful in the Sino-Soviet dispute and at the same time provide tempting opportunities for using Cuba as a base to advance the political interests of the party in Central and South America.

The KGB leaders could be expected to think of the leverage the new strategic balance would bring, especially on the problem of Berlin and Germany, and so many of them would probably favor the proposal. Although what the bureaucracies dealing with foreign affairs thought would be of little importance to the leadership, they would welcome the move for the same reasons.

What the regional party apparatchiks and local government officials thought would also be of little concern to the top leaders, but the apparatchiks would probably find the idea of sending missiles to Cuba appealing because it offered the prospect of avoiding a cutback in consumer goods, permitting both guns and butter.

As for ideologues at all levels, "hard-liners" could be expected to see the decision as appropriate to their view of the world. Doctrinaire ideologists would see it as foiling the "imperialists" who would otherwise inevitably and ruthlessly exploit the strategic situation posed by the fact that the United States had so many more nuclear ICBMs than the Soviets.

THE METHODS OF ANALYSIS IN PRACTICE

As it happened, during the Cuban missile crisis two groups of U.S. government officials actually did use what amounted to this kind of "political process" mode of analysis. The first were Sovietologists in the State Department's Bureau of Intelligence and Research (INR), whose memo analyzing the Soviet motives was mentioned in Chapter 1. This memo began with a proposition expressly recognizing multiple power centers with differing motives:

> As with the major policy decisions of all governments, whether dictatorial or democratic, different segments of the Soviet leadership undoubtedly saw particular advantages and disadvantages in putting missiles in Cuba according to their own parochial interests and responsibilities.

Thus the motive for the decision, the memo argued, was strategic in the broad sense that a general improvement in the Soviet military position would affect the entire political context, strengthening the Soviet hand for dealing with the whole range of problems facing it and unanticipated problems as well. But even though general rather than specific security and foreign policy goals were the principal motive of the Soviet decision to deploy missiles to Cuba, the memo argued, once the deployment was accomplished, it promised enticing prospects for specific gains in foreign policy and ancillary benefits that would appeal to various segments of the Soviet leadership.

If the move in Cuba was successful and the overall Soviet position strengthened, Soviet leverage on Berlin would indeed be improved. The memo also made the point that NATO would surely be shaken and the chances of the United States successfully creating a multi-lateral nuclear force, which was at the time being discussed within NATO, would be greatly reduced.

In Latin America, the memo argued, other potential "Castros" would be encouraged. American power would be less impressive and American protection less desirable, and some of the Latin American states would move in the Soviet direction even if their governments were not actually overthrown.

In Asia, the memo continued, a successful move in Cuba would cut the ground from under the Chinese Communists and go far toward convincing Communists everywhere that Soviet leadership was strong and Soviet methods in dealing with the "imperialists" effective.

To sum up, the State Department Sovietologists argued that several of the top leaders from the party, the KGB, and the military were involved in the Soviet decision. Each of these leaders shared an interest in the strategic goals of the Soviet state. But each of them interpreted those goals somewhat differently, and each of them also had goals of his own.

KENNEDY AND THE EXCOM

The second group who used a political process approach was Kennedy and the members of the ExCom—once they finished trying to figure out the motives behind the decision to deploy the missiles to Cuba and started devising their moves to meet the crisis as it progressed.

When they were engaged in trying to decide what motives lay behind the Soviet deployment of missiles to Cuba, Kennedy and the ExCom thought of the Soviet Union as monolithic—a "black box" that acted to maximize the power of the state. But when they began to devise a policy to deal with the situation, they unconsciously shifted to a "political process" mode of thinking. Quite clearly they envisioned their opponents as individual human beings and groups of human beings working within different organizations. Kennedy repeatedly said that the U.S. moves should be gradual and paced so as to avoid backing the Soviet leaders into a corner or placing them in a position where they might have what he called a "spasm reaction." Consideration was given at each stage of the effect the move under discussion would have on the military, the KGB, and the party leaders. The hope was to strengthen the hand of those power centers likely to favor negotiations and accommodation and weaken the hand of the power centers likely to oppose them—so far as it was possible for U.S. moves to have these effects.

The first point to note is that an analysis using this political process approach did in fact resolve one puzzlement created by assuming that states, including the Soviet Union, are monolithic. This is the internal inconsistency between the goal of trying to overcome the "missile gap in reverse" and the presumed goal of probing the will of the West and the new American president. In the political process analysis, this puzzlement just disappeared. In such an analysis, probing the will of the West was not a consideration. It would be highly unlikely that such disparate centers of power would all be interested in probing the will of the West, but they would be very likely to share the "state" goal of wanting to right the imbalance in missiles, even if the measures to do so were partial and temporary. Sending the IRBMs and MRBMs to Cuba to right the strategic balance was a credible motive, but sending them to probe the will of the West was not.

At the same time, the fact that IRBMs and MRBMs did not solve the problem of the missile imbalance in any permanent sense was at least partly explained. Although the MRBMs would not solve the problem permanently, they would give the military and the other "hawks" some satisfaction because the MRBMs and IRBMs would at least, in the words of the American National Intelligence Estimate (NIE), "begin to degrade the American second-strike capability."

So the puzzlement created by the fact that deploying the missiles to Cuba did not completely solve the problem of missile imbalance was also solved. There was something attractive to deploying the missiles to Cuba for each of the three most important of the power centers in the Soviet Union. The hawks got at least part of a loaf if not a full half; those concerned about the economic consequences of a crash ICBM program got a stretched-out buildup in ICBMs; those concerned about the effects on consumers got butter as well as guns;

and those concerned with China and Latin America saw enticing opportunities.

It is also worth noting that to the extent that a political process analysis was the more sophisticated mode of analysis and more likely to lead to policies that would achieve the desired ends, the policy actually followed by the Kennedy administration of blockading Cuba and negotiating rather than bombing the missile sites in a "surgical first strike" was by far the better policy. For to the extent that the political process analysis was correct, the basic Soviet motives were not in fact belligerent or aggressive per se. The "state" goal was defensive, to correct the missile imbalance, and the other motives of the action flowed from an attempt to reconcile the disagreements among the Soviets' own contending factions.

NOTES

1. Much of what follows in this and the following chapters is drawn from my private papers in the Kennedy Library, which were accumulated during the crisis in my capacity as the director of intelligence and research in the Department of State. These papers are described in more detail in my *To Move a Nation: The Politics of Foreign Policy in the Administration of John F. Kennedy* (Garden City, NY: Doubleday, 1967). Another major source has been two recently published collections of declassified government documents dealing with the crisis. These are Laurence Chang and Peter Kornbluh, *The Cuban Missile Crisis, 1962: A National Security Archive Reader* (New York: The New Press, 1992), and Mary S. McAuliffe, ed., *CIA Documents on the Cuban Missile Crisis, 1962* (Washington, DC: History Staff, Central Intelligence Agency, October, 1992). The Kennedy Library has also recently released tapes of meetings of the ExCom and of one of President Kennedy's sessions with members of Congress.

I have also drawn on Arthur M. Schlesinger, Jr., *A Thousand Days: John F. Kennedy in the White House* (Boston: Houghton-Mifflin, 1965); Theodore C. Sorensen, *Kennedy* (New York: Harper and Row, 1965); Graham T. Allison, *Essence of Decision: Explaining the Cuban Missile Crisis* (Boston: Little, Brown, 1971); Raymond L. Garthoff, *Reflections on the Cuban Missile Crisis* (Washington, DC: The Brookings Institution, 1987); McGeorge

Bundy, *Danger and Survival: Choices about the Bomb in the First Fifty Years* (New York: Random House, 1988); and McGeorge Bundy, transcriber, James G. Blight, ed., "October 27, 1962: Transcripts of the Meetings of the ExComm," *International Security* (Winter 1987/88).

2. In his memoirs, Khrushchev says flatly that the Jupiters in Turkey and Italy "were already obsolete." See Strobe Talbot, translator and editor, *Khrushchev Remembers: The Last Testament* (Boston: Little, Brown, 1974), p. 512.

3. In an article entitled "The Cuban Missile Crisis: Trading the Jupiters in Turkey?" *Political Science Quarterly* (Spring, 1980), Barton J. Bernstein makes much of the fact that although the decision to deploy the Jupiter missiles to Turkey was made in the Eisenhower administration they did not actually get to Turkey until after the beginning of the Kennedy administration. He also suggests that Kennedy did not *order* the missiles out of Turkey, "but only implied a study of its feasibility."

Bernstein's conclusions are naive. Presidents rarely order moves that go back on a previous president's promise to an Ally, and they certainly never do so without consulting the Ally. Kennedy made his desire to withdraw the Jupiter missiles from Turkey very clear on three occasions at which I was present in my then capacity as the director of the State Department's Bureau of Intelligence and Research. But Kennedy understood that the timing of the withdrawal would depend on the attitude of the Turks. The Turkish government had obtained the approval of their parliament only with difficulty and were reluctant to bring the subject up so soon. They argued that the U.S. government should wait to withdraw the missiles until such time as one or two of the Polaris missile submarines could be put on station in the Mediterranean. No decision was actually made to wait until that time, but this does seem to account for the fact that the State Department did not push the matter as vigorously as the president felt they should have.

Another writer, Donald L. Hafner, in "Bureaucratic Politics and 'Those Frigging Missiles': JFK, Cuba and U.S. Missiles in Turkey," *Orbis* (Summer, 1977) talks about the "myth" that Kennedy was "shocked and surprised" to find that his instructions about getting the Jupiters out of Turkey had "not been executed by State Department bureaucrats," because this left the United States vulnerable to pressure from the Soviets to make a "deal" about removing the

American missiles in Turkey in exchange for removing the Soviet missiles from Cuba.

Here the writer misses the point. Kennedy knew as well as the rest of the people involved that the American missiles were still in Turkey. Kennedy was not shocked and surprised. He was *angry*. He was angry because the delay in getting the missiles out of Turkey left the United States vulnerable to pressure to do something that would shake the NATO alliance.

4. This discussion of the classical, traditional, or black box mode of analysis and the discussion below of the political process mode of analysis are drawn from my *The Politics of Policy Making in Defense and Foreign Affairs: Conceptual Models and Bureaucratic Politics,* 3rd ed. (Englewood Cliffs, NJ: Prentice Hall, 1993). Others who have written on the subject are Richard E. Neustadt, Gabriel A. Almond, Charles E. Lindblom, Warner R. Schilling, Samuel P. Huntington, Graham T. Allison, Morton H. Halperin, I. M. Destler, Alexander L. George, and Robert J. Art. For a comparison and analysis of the works of all these authors, see Robert J. Art, "Bureaucratic Politics and American Foreign Policy: A Critique," *Policy Sciences* (December, 1974).

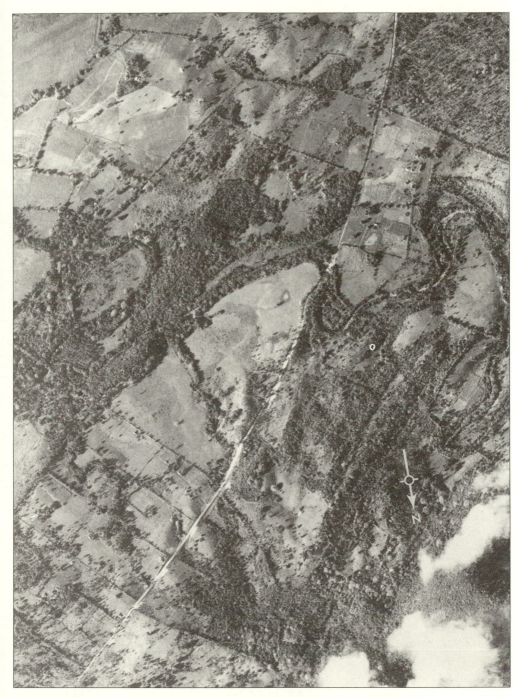

Future MRBM Site at San Cristóbal, late August, 1962

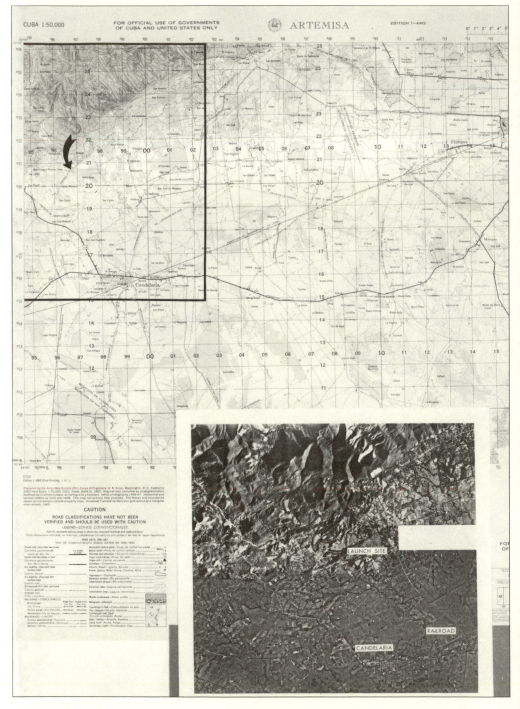

MRBM Site at San Cristóbal

MRBM Site at San Cristóbal, mid-October, 1962

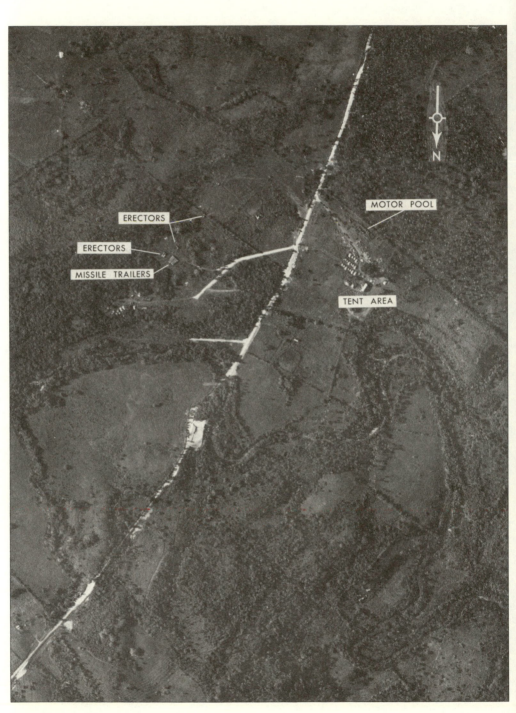

MRBM Site at San Cristóbal, 24 hours later

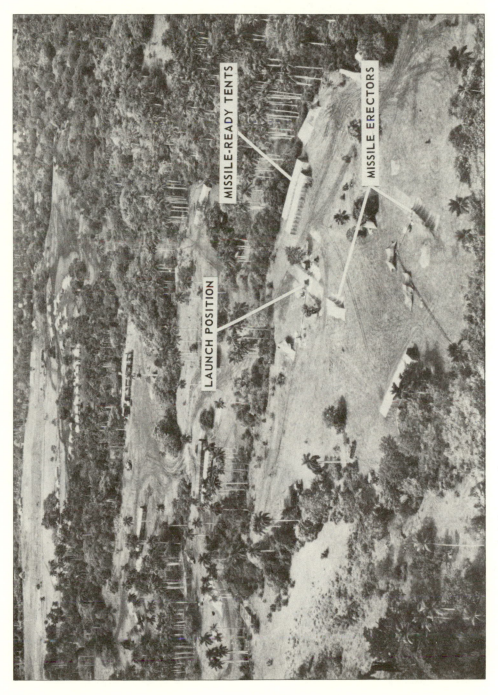

MRBM Site at San Cristóbal, late October

Future IRBM Site at Guanajay, late August

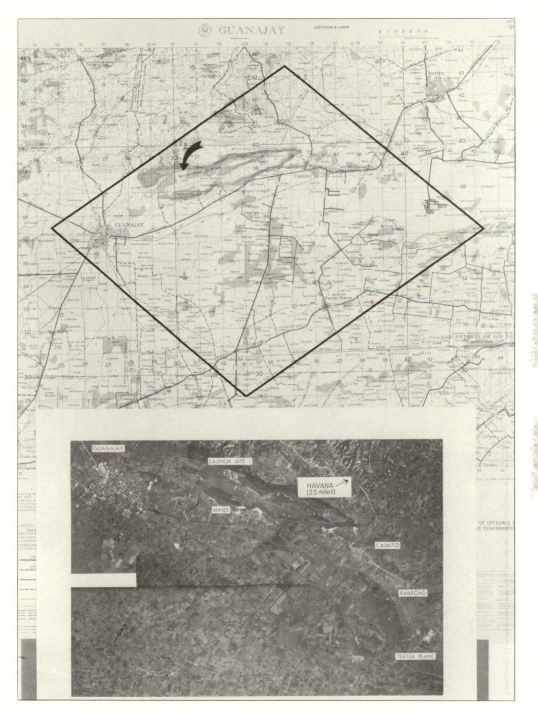

IRBM Site at Guanajay

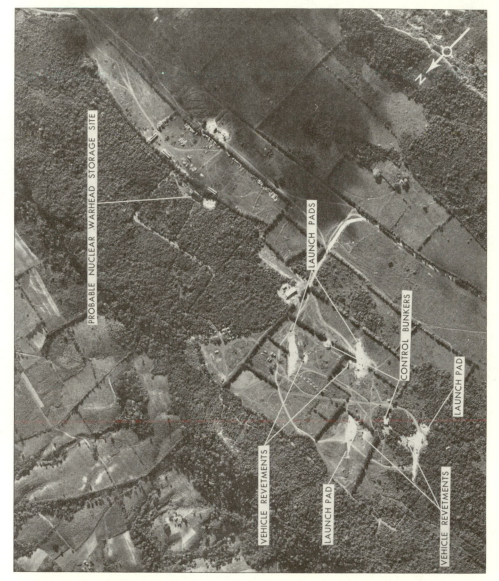

IRBM Site at Guanajay, mid-October

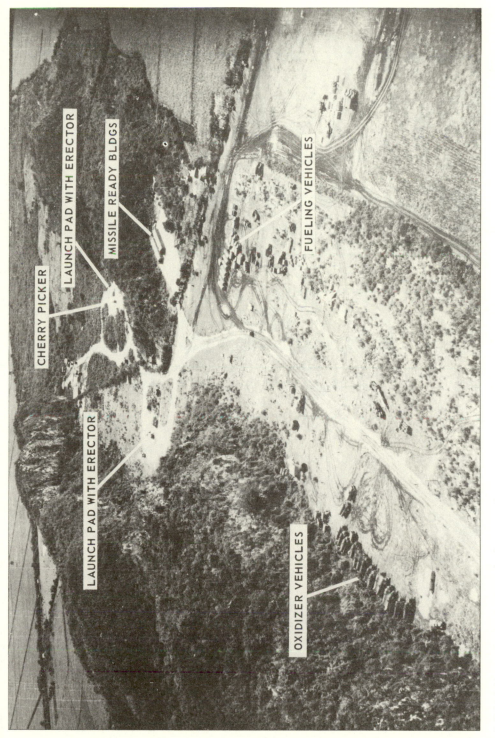

CHERRY PICKER

LAUNCH PAD WITH ERECTOR

MISSILE READY BLDGS

LAUNCH PAD WITH ERECTOR

FUELING VEHICLES

OXIDIZER VEHICLES

MRBM Site at Sagua La Grande, late October

Chapter 6

The Policy Decisions

In their analysis of why the Soviets had put the missiles in Cuba, the members of the ExCom were mainly in agreement. But when it came time to decide what to do about the Soviet missiles in Cuba, opinions differed sharply.

Initially the discussion focused on the proposal to take out the Soviet missiles with a "surgical air strike." The most powerful argument for this course of action assumed that the missiles had not yet become operational. If none of the missiles was operational, taking them out by a surprise bombing ran no risk that a local commander would fire a missile on his own responsibility or in panic.

But even if the missiles were not yet operational, bombing them would run some risk that the Soviets would retaliate with missiles based in the Soviet Union itself. Most members of the ExCom believed this kind of all-out response was highly unlikely. But the Soviets might well respond by bombing the American Jupiters in Turkey—or even the Jupiters based in Italy and the Thors based in Great Britain.

Alternatively, the Soviet response to bombing the missile sites in

Cuba might also be simply to seize Berlin. What would the United States do then?

Rather than bomb the missiles, one group of ExCom members wanted the United States to blockade Cuba to ensure that no more missiles could be landed and to couple this blockade with efforts to reach a negotiated settlement that would require the missiles already in Cuba to be withdrawn.

Again, the Soviet response might simply be to seize Berlin. Or their response might be a sort of tit for tat—not to seize Berlin but to blockade it—and this time, unlike the earlier blockade that the Allies met with a massive airlift, to include some sort of air blockade.

Suppose the United States confined its reaction to diplomatic and political moves? If so, any subsequent Soviet attempt to repeat the challenge in an important place such as Berlin would mean that the U.S. reaction the second time around would have to be violent precisely because it had shown weakness in Cuba. It is axiomatic that the second time around the victim nation will be impelled not to repeat its weakness.

U.S. OBJECTIVES

If the principal Soviet objective in putting missiles into Cuba was strategic in its broadest political sense, so was the American objective in getting them out. But beyond this, the discussion of American objectives in the ExCom meetings and throughout Washington inevitably merged with the discussion of the alternative means that might be used to accomplish these objectives.

The United States could tolerate a gradual evening out of the strategic equation between the United States and the Soviet Union—so long as the evening out took several years and so permitted political adjustments as it proceeded and at least tacit understandings, if not formal ones, on a whole range of matters including arms control. What the United States could not accept was a swift, sudden, and secret shift in the strategic equation. Such a shift would be unsettling to the whole range of issues between the East and the West, and unacceptably so. Thus first and foremost, the American objective was to have the Soviet missiles removed from Cuba.

The United States, of course, would also have liked to see the end of the Soviet military presence in Cuba and the end of Castro's regime. But here is where the importance of means began to be felt. The full panoply of American military power was appropriate to getting the missiles out of Cuba—and it might well have turned out to be necessary. But at what point as one descends the ladder of objectives and they become less vital to American survival itself does military power begin to be inappropriate, entailing political costs greater than the possible military gains?

For example, at one point during the crisis we in the State Department intelligence bureau wrote a memo suggesting that the United States should demand not only that the Soviet missiles be removed from Cuba but that Castro and his regime should also be removed. Castro had been an annoyance before, but now that he had either asked for Soviet missiles or granted permission for their deployment, he had become more than an annoyance. With a certain tartness, President Kennedy told me that while Castro had been troublesome to the United States, the missiles were a threat to its very existence. To make Castro's removal one of the American goals would be a distraction, in some circumstances perhaps even a fatal distraction. The United States must focus single-mindedly on the one issue that really mattered, the presence of the missiles in Cuba. Kennedy was right, of course, and none of us in the intelligence bureau ever mentioned removing Castro again!

So the main goal was getting rid of the missiles, and thereafter the discussions focused almost exclusively on that problem.

The possibility that the Soviets had put the missiles in Cuba to trade them for the missiles in Turkey had already been discussed and dismissed. But perhaps a trade would give the Soviets a fig leaf for the decision to pull their missiles out of Cuba. But how could that be managed without letting Khrushchev claim that it was the United States that caused the crisis by Eisenhower's decision to put the Jupiters in Turkey?

The decision to put the Jupiter missiles in Turkey and Italy and the Thors in Great Britain had been made at the request of NATO during the Eisenhower administration as a response to the Soviet's deployment of MRBMs and IRBMs aimed at Western Europe. Kennedy had long since made up his mind that these missiles were not only useless but provocative. The missiles in Turkey were the most provocative, and he had raised the question of removing them at an NSC meeting shortly after his inauguration. But the Berlin crisis had intervened. In May, 1962, Kennedy instructed Rusk to raise the question with the Turks. But the Turks objected that after the effort they had made to persuade their parliament to give its approval, they did not want to have to go back to it so soon to ask permission to have them removed. Why not wait, the Turks argued, until the first of the Polaris submarines could be stationed in the Mediterranean? That would give the Turkish government a plausible excuse for going back to the parliament.

Early in the summer of 1962, Kennedy raised the question again, and in August, 1962, he rejected the State Department's case for further delay and directed that steps be taken immediately to persuade the Turks to let the missiles be removed.

Then the Soviet missiles appeared in Cuba. To remove the American missiles in Turkey voluntarily was one thing, but to remove them under the threat of Soviet missiles in Cuba was an entirely different matter. Removing them under threat would do serious and long-lasting damage to NATO. Furthermore, since the decision to put the Jupiters in Turkey and Italy had been a NATO decision, a decision to remove them would also have to be a NATO decision. The United States could not remove the missiles from Turkey unilaterally.

An important difference between the U.S. deployment of missiles to Turkey, Italy, and the United Kingdom and the Soviet deployment of missiles to Cuba was the manner in which the two different deployments had been made. First, as already mentioned, the American missiles had been deployed in response to a threat from the Soviet Union—the large-scale deployment of their missiles in the western part of the Soviet Union aimed at Western Europe. Second, the impetus for sending the American missiles to Turkey, Italy, and the United Kingdom came not from the United States, but from the European countries threatened by the Soviet missiles. Third, the decision had been openly debated for two years. It had finally been made not only at the urging of the countries concerned but with their full and public agreement. Finally, the deployment had been publicly announced and carried out.

Although Castro and the Soviets justified their actions after the crisis on the grounds of an American threat to Cuba, they never suggested that it was a nuclear threat requiring nuclear defenses, as the Soviet deployment of missiles in the western Soviet Union had been. What is more, both the Soviet decision and its deployment of the missiles were secret.

Kennedy made it clear to the Soviets and the world that once the problem of Soviet missiles in Cuba was solved, the United States would be happy to negotiate the removal of the American missiles not only in Turkey but in Italy and the United Kingdom. But, he insisted, since the American missiles had been deployed in response to Soviet missiles aimed at Europe, an American withdrawal could be made only in the context of a disarmament agreement applying to both Eastern and Western Europe.

At the same time Kennedy recognized that trading the missiles in Turkey for those in Cuba was better than a war, and he took steps to make a missiles-in-Turkey for missiles-in-Cuba trade less harmful politically if such a "deal" turned out to be the only way to avoid war. Unbeknownst to anyone in the ExCom except Rusk and probably his brother, Robert, President Kennedy asked Rusk to lay the groundwork for a deal. As Rusk revealed in 1987, Kennedy had him contact Columbia University Dean Andrew W. Cordier, who had until recently been an undersecretary at the UN. When and if Kennedy requested it, Cordier would arrange to have U Thant, the secretary general, "request" both the Soviet Union and the United States to bring back, to their own territory, all missiles stationed outside their own borders.[1] A general withdrawal by both sides at the request of the UN would enormously reduce the political effect on NATO. The United States could have magnanimously agreed, while pointing out—and documenting the fact—that Kennedy had much earlier been moving unilaterally to remove the missiles from Turkey.

The ExCom discussions on Wednesday, October 17, examined the whole range of alternatives, but sentiment seemed to be strongest for bombing the missiles with a "surgical" air strike. Another possible "surgical" operation might be a *coup de main* by parachute forces.

General Walter C. Sweeney, the commander of the air forces that would carry out an air strike, said that if that was the decision, he could not promise to destroy more than 90 percent of the missiles in a surprise attack. Also, it was always possible that the U–2s had not identified all of the missile sites. One or two might have been missed.

In either case a surgical strike could be considered *only* if none of the missiles were operational. If any of the missiles were operational, to repeat, some local Soviet commander might panic, assume that the big war was on with the Soviet Union itself under attack, and take matters into his own hands.

But the point was quickly made that even if none of the missiles were operational, a surprise attack would leave the United States with a moral stigma for the rest of time. The Soviets would have solid evidence to support the propaganda thesis that the United States would some day begin World War III by launching a surprise attack on the Soviet Union. The only way to avoid this moral stigma would be to give advance warning. But warning would permit preparations and defensive measures that would make an attack less likely to succeed. It would also permit the Soviet Union to muster world opinion, with the very possible result that any action to remove the missiles, political or military, would be frustrated.

As the discussion proceeded on October 18 and 19, the idea of a "surgical" strike began to look less and less promising, with or without warning. For one thing, as McGeorge Bundy pointed out, a blockade is much easier to manage than an air strike.

An even weightier consideration was that the Joint Chiefs of Staff became more and more insistent that the bombing could not be limited to just the missile sites without risks that they regarded as unacceptable. Castro's planes, the artillery batteries opposite Guantánamo, potential nuclear storage sites, lines of communication—all of these would have to be eliminated in that first strike.

But even then the attack might not be completely successful, with or without advance warning. To be absolutely certain of success, the bombing would have to be followed by an invasion. The JCS invasion plan called for 1,190 air strikes the very first day, and probably just as many would have to be mounted each day thereafter until the island was occupied. The damage to the Cuban population and to the Cuban economy would be extensive.

Assembling the necessary forces for an invasion would also take time, and each day that passed increased the chances that at least the MRBMs would become operational. But the whole purpose of a preemptive strike, with or without warning, was to prevent the missiles from becoming operational.

To more and more of the members of the ExCom the trouble with an air strike was not only that it offered no guarantee that it would be successful but that prudence demanded that the effort be expanded—bombing more than just the sites, adding an invasion force, and so on.

There was also the question of a Soviet response. If the United States chose the sudden, violent course of knocking out the missiles, the Soviets would probably feel compelled to do something equally dramatic and drastic. The most likely Soviet response seemed to be a retaliatory bombing of the Jupiter bases in Turkey—a further widening and escalation of the conflict.

Those who favored an air strike argued that a blockade might keep additional missiles from getting to Cuba but that it would do nothing whatsoever to force the Soviets to remove the missiles that were already there. For a time no one had an answer to that argument. The vision of the Soviets refusing to withdraw the missiles and the blockade continuing for months or years was disheartening.

In response to the idea that a blockade might drag on and on, those who opposed an air strike and favored a blockade began to argue that a blockade would be only the first step. If the combination of a blockade and negotiations failed to persuade the Soviets to remove the missiles already there, the United States could then consider other options.

The first step up the ladder would be to include not just weapons in the blockade, but oil and all kinds of imports except food and medicine. If that did not persuade the Soviets to withdraw the missiles, then the United States could consider other kinds of pressure, eventually working up to an air strike or an invasion or both.

Also, even though a blockade would do nothing *directly* to pressure the Soviets to take out the missiles already there, it would generate some significant indirect pressure. A blockade would send a signal to the rest of the world that the United States took the Soviet Union's deployment of nuclear missiles to Cuba very seriously. If the Soviets were intransigent, the tension would alarm governments everywhere in the world, and they would add their own pressure on the Soviets to withdraw the missiles.

Quite clearly world opinion would want the missiles out, and the Soviets were not indifferent to world opinion. It was at least conceivable that under the pressure of world opinion some of the Soviet leaders would favor a discreet withdrawal.

Still another factor was the Soviet preoccupation with secrecy and a fear that the United States might learn some of their missile secrets by seizing one of their ships. As President Kennedy himself said on TV on December 17 after the crisis was over, the quarantine "had much more power than we first thought it did, because I think the Soviet Union was very reluctant to have us stop ships which carried with them a good deal of their highly secret and sensitive material."

Only one Soviet ship challenged the quarantine by proceeding on to Cuba, and the fact that this ship was an oil tanker and so not capable of carrying secret weapons tends to support Kennedy's argument.

Thus by Thursday evening, October 18, a consensus seemed to be developing around the idea of a blockade against offensive weapons as a first step—in McNamara's phrase, maintaining the "options" of raising the level of the blockade to include oil and other goods, of launching an air strike, or of mounting an invasion if increases in the level of pressure proved necessary. Before the day was over, the president had indicated his own preference for a blockade.

Not that a blockade was free of drawbacks. The first was what a number of administration officials had said in the debate that had begun in August—that a blockade was contrary to international law, that it was in fact an act of war. But it was noted that a rather different light would be put on a blockade if the Organization of American States, the OAS, voted in favor of it.

The other trouble, already mentioned, was that a blockade did not address itself directly to the question of the Soviet missiles that were already *in* Cuba. A blockade did not *remove* the missiles; it only prevented a further buildup.

In addition, a blockade meant that American ships would intercept Soviet ships, stop them, and demand that they submit themselves to the humiliation of being boarded for inspection. If the Soviet ships refused to stop or submit to boarding, it would, like an air strike, put the Americans in the position of firing the first shot.

The great advantage of a blockade, on the other hand, was that it began at the very lowest level in the use of force and permitted a step-by-step progression up the ladder of coercion, giving the Soviets repeated opportunities to consider again the choice of withdrawing the missiles and making a settlement. It permitted events to be paced. It provided time—time between steps for each side to consider the next step and the possible consequences of that next step. It kept at a minimum, in President Kennedy's phrase, the possibility of a "spasm reaction."

One major obstacle—not objection, but obstacle—to a blockade was that the JCS still wanted an air strike or an invasion. The president met with the chiefs on Friday morning and came out of the meeting visibly annoyed. He again repeated his preference for a blockade and at this time supplied the word *quarantine* to describe it.

The word *quarantine* had obvious political advantages both at home and abroad. At home, it was reminiscent of President Roosevelt's "quarantining the aggressors" speech in support of the Allies in the very early days of World War II. Abroad, it struck a less belligerent note than the word *blockade*. But before departing for the trip to Cleveland and Chicago, already described, Kennedy also made it clear that his decision was still tentative.

It seems likely that the president was waiting to make his decision final mainly because of the continued opposition of the JCS to a blockade and their preference for more violent action. It was clear that some of the memoranda being written were not so much to present this or that case to the president—since he had already heard them all—but to build a record. If something went wrong, many of these memoranda would obviously be leaked to the Congress and the press. Any alternative the president chose was chancy, at best, and it is elementary prudence for a president to protect himself from the charge that he had overruled his military advisers on a "military" issue.

Kennedy wanted to make very, very sure that all the participants felt that they had had a full opportunity to make their views known. Because of the possibility that some might be inhibited from speaking their minds fully in front of the president, Kennedy arranged for a special meeting of the ExCom on Friday evening when he would *not* be present.

John McCone marshaled the arguments against a blockade—the legal difficulties, the fact that a blockade might prevent other missiles from being brought in but would do nothing to get those out that were already there, and so on. Everyone present agreed that a public warning followed by an attack would probably end up in disaster. But the "hawks" presented the case for an attack without warning with considerable force.

The consensus for a blockade that had seemed to be developing on Thursday began to come apart. It fell to Robert Kennedy to present the case not so much for a blockade, but against an attack without warning, and he did so just as forcefully as those that had made the case in favor. "For the United States to attack a small country without warning," he said, "would irreparably hurt our reputation in the world—and our own conscience." A sudden surprise attack would be morally reprehensible, he argued, in violation of American traditions and ideals. In wrenching words that moved everyone present, Robert Kennedy said that he did not want America to commit the "infamy" of a Pearl Harbor. He did not want his brother "to be the Tojo of American history."

Robert Kennedy's eloquent plea seemed to convince the waverers that a blockade ought to be at least the first step—even though it would be, in McGeorge Bundy's phrase, a "slow agony."

It seems clear that both the president and his brother were acutely conscious not only that the missiles had to be removed—God willing without the use of force—but also that this was the first nuclear crisis the world had ever faced, and that what the United States did to meet this crisis would set precedents for future crises and perhaps the entire era.

On Saturday, October 20, President Kennedy said that before making the final decision on a quarantine, he wanted to talk personally with the Air Force Tactical Bombing Command to make very sure that a limited air strike could not guarantee 100 percent success. The meeting took place on Sunday, October 21, and it was at this time that Kennedy learned from the intelligence people that it was really too late to be sure that a few of the MRBMs were not ready to fire. Later evidence indicated that some of the MRBMs were indeed ready to fire by October 21 and that *all* of them were ready to fire by October 27.

Those in the ExCom who still had misgivings about a quarantine were given one more chance. Mindful of the need to have their support, Kennedy stressed, even as he announced that he had decided upon a quarantine, that the choices of an air strike or an invasion would still be open if the quarantine did not work. Those whose proposals were not chosen, he joked, were the lucky ones, for they could say, "I told you so."

On Sunday afternoon the president began going over the "disclosure" speech Sorensen had been working on for the past few days and all through the preceding night. The speech went through several drafts, and many different people were asked for their comments.

It was at this point that the INR analysis, mentioned above, of the conversations between Bowles and Dobrynin, Khrushchev and Kohler, and Gromyko and President Kennedy became relevant. The key elements of the analysis were as follows:

> ... A systematic Soviet effort to avoid making the Cuban buildup the subject of a direct US-Soviet confrontation has impressed us as an important element in these conversations. ...

... While it may be true that Dobrynin was genuinely un-
aware of the Soviet deployment, he appears to have been under
instructions to seek out and report information on US views of
the Cuban situation. . . .

... Khrushchev personally ... must have been aware that
the US knew about the Soviet missiles. . . .

We believe that the tenor of the Gromyko and Khrushchev
conversations suggests an attempt to avoid a direct confrontation with the United States over the issue of missile deployments in Cuba.

Moscow may well hope to avoid becoming overly committed
to counteractions which it may not wish to take in response to
vigorous US response to the Cuban buildup, and thus leave its
hands free for negotiation and, if faced with extreme danger of
war, for withdrawal with the least loss of face.

Implications for US Policy

We believe that US policy should take into account this ap-
parent Soviet desire to avoid a direct US-Soviet confrontation
on the Cuban issue.

In words: Our public statements should be keyed to Cuban
irresponsibility in obtaining offensive weapons rather than to
the Soviet role in providing them.

In deeds: We believe that a blockade should not be directed
exclusively at the USSR which ships arms but should be broad-
ened to include petroleum (and perhaps other products)
shipped by non-bloc countries.

If direct military action against Cuba becomes necessary, we
should avoid singling out Soviet manned installations for attack.

The copy of this memo in the files of the secretary of state shows
that Rusk underlined the following phrases:

"A systematic Soviet effort to avoid making the Cuban buildup
the subject of a direct US-Soviet confrontation, . . ."

". . . he [Dobrynin] appears to have been under instructions to
seek out and report information on US views of the Cuban
situation."

". . . Khrushchev personally . . . must have been aware that the
US knew about the Soviet missiles."

"Moscow may well hope to avoid becoming overly committed to counteractions. . . ."

". . . we should avoid singling out Soviet manned installations for attack."

The overall thrust of the memo was that the United States should take a firm and determined stance, but take care at the same time to leave the Soviets a way out. Quite independently, both Averell Harriman and Llewellyn Thompson, drawing on their experience as ambassadors to the Soviet Union, stressed the same point. And it was the president's natural preference.

The president had decided on Friday that Monday evening would be the time of disclosure. Preparations were already in full swing, with much to be done. Resolutions for the UN and the Organization of American States had to be drafted. Special arrangements had to be made to brief our major Allies. Presidential letters had to be prepared for 43 heads of government, and messages had to be sent to all our posts overseas explaining our action. The congressional leadership had to be informed. The Pentagon had to alert the Strategic Air Command, assemble the quarantine forces, and prepare the troops needed for an invasion if that should become necessary.

At the State Department, U. Alexis Johnson, the deputy under secretary for political affairs, was the man chosen to coordinate the "scenario"—a schedule of who was to do what and when, all keyed to "P-hour," seven o'clock Monday evening, when the president was to give his speech ("P" for "public" after someone discovered that the original designation had a special meaning in nuclear war planning). For Monday, October 22, the scenario read as follows:

9:00 a.m., Monday, October 22—ExCom meeting

10:00—Lawrence O'Brien [presidential assistant for congressional relations] to notify congressional leadership

12:00 noon—The president's press secretary, Pierre Salinger, to announce time of president's speech

3:00 p.m.—National Security Council meeting, followed by Cabinet meeting

5:00—The president, Rusk, McNamara, and McCone to brief congressional leadership

6:00—Ambassador Dobrynin of the Soviet Union to see Secretary Rusk

6:15—Under Secretary George Ball and Director of Intelligence Roger Hilsman to brief 46 Allied ambassadors

7:00—The president's speech

7:30—Assistant Secretary Edwin Martin to brief Latin American ambassadors

8:00—Rusk and Hilsman to brief "neutral nations" ambassadors

—Ball, Alexis Johnson, and Abram Chayes (the legal adviser of the State Department) to give first half of press briefing

8:15—Hilsman to give second half of press briefing

After checking over the preparations at a final meeting on Sunday, Rusk sighed wearily and suggested that everyone ought to get as much rest as they could. "By this time tomorrow, gentlemen," he said, "we will be in a flaming crisis." All there was left to do was wait—and hope that nothing leaked that would give the Soviets a chance to take the initiative away from us.

THE PROBLEM OF A LEAK

Miraculously, the secret held—but just barely. All through the weekend Washington was taut with the sense of crisis. Too many high officials had canceled social engagements or were called away from them. Too many people were at the office too early and stayed too late. Too many lights were burning at the State Department and the Pentagon at odd hours. By Saturday afternoon the Washington press corps knew something unusual was up and by Sunday they were frantic with curiosity. Most of the reporters accredited to the State Department and the Pentagon spent Sunday there, prowling the corridors looking for some lead.

Many reporters thought the Soviet Union might have delivered an ultimatum on Berlin; others thought the United States might have finally lost patience with Castro. A fluke question—were we planning an invasion of Cuba?—permitted Arthur Sylvester, the assistant secretary of public affairs at the Pentagon, to justify a quibble, and he said "No" with some emphasis, since what was being planned was a quarantine. This turned attention away from Cuba and toward Berlin for a time and served as a useful smoke screen.

Quite independently, both the *New York Times* and the *Washington Post* assembled a group of reporters to "brainstorm" what might be going on. Both groups decided that the crisis concerned either Cuba or Berlin. Each reporter then phoned officials he knew: "We have learned that a crisis is brewing in Berlin, and that . . ." or, "We have learned that the Soviet arms shipments to Cuba have reached such proportions that the United States feels it must launch an invasion." Most of the officials who were called tried to head off a wrong and alarming story—"Oh, no, that is not the problem at all!" But in the process each of them gave out one or two bits of true information. So by Sunday evening, both the *New York Times* and the *Washington Post* had most of the story.

The president telephoned the publishers of both papers and asked them to hold off until after his talk to the nation on Monday—since publication before his talk would give the Soviets warning and an opportunity to present the United States with an ultimatum. Both newspapers promptly agreed, although the *Times*—irresponsibly— did publish a story about an "air of crisis" linked to a "new development in Cuba that cannot be disclosed at this point."

A few last-minute details had to be ironed out, and unscheduled meetings were sandwiched in. Legal details, details about military questions, details about Stevenson's speech at the UN—all needed to be checked with the president at one stage or another.

My own problem was the intelligence briefing I was to give the ambassadors. It had to be convincing, for we would need support. We would be presenting our case to the Organization of American States at the outset, and we might soon need much more than political support from our Allies. And it would be helpful if we had at least the sympathy of the "neutrals." But even so, there was considerable reluctance in the intelligence community to let me use the U–2 pictures in briefing the ambassadors.

The problem was not one of publicly admitting that we had been overflying Cuba, for we actually had some legal basis for the more recent U–2 surveillance. On October 3 a communiqué issued by the Inter-American Foreign Ministers Conference had condemned secret military preparations in the hemisphere, and, pointing directly at Cuba, went on to say that it was "desirable to intensify individual and collective surveillance of the delivery of arms and implements of war and all other items of strategic importance to the Communist regime of Cuba."

The problem was that the intelligence community was afraid of revealing too much about intelligence methods and techniques and especially the high quality of photography achieved by the U–2 camera systems—in spite of the fact that the Soviets had learned a great deal about the quality of U–2 photography after they shot down Gary Powers. I met twice that day with the president to work it out, once at eleven in the morning in a very small meeting in his office at which Stevenson's presentation to the UN was also discussed, and again in the very large meeting at three in the afternoon that reviewed the whole scenario. The president decided that the pictures had to be used and within the next few days they should also be released to the general public.

There was a bad scare just six hours before the president's speech. The Soviet mission to the United Nations announced early Monday afternoon that they would shortly have an important statement. Plans were quickly laid to announce the quarantine right away— but the "important statement" was merely Gromyko's departure speech.

FIVE P.M.—CONGRESSIONAL BRIEFING

The congressional meeting began with an intelligence briefing. After McCone and an aide had finished, the president began to talk. He explained why an air strike or an invasion would be unwise, emphasizing that the quarantine was only the first step. An invasion might soon become necessary, but it would take still another week to assemble the forces, and in the meantime it was essential to stop the Soviets from bringing in more equipment to make the missile bases fully operational.

Senator Richard B. Russell of Georgia, chairman of the Senate Armed Services Committee, urged an immediate invasion. A quarantine would take time and thus increase the risk. As for warning and striking the first blow, President Kennedy's speeches and the congressional resolution putting the Soviets on notice that the United States would not tolerate offensive bases in Cuba were ample warning; and it was the Soviets who had struck the first blow by putting the missiles in Cuba. Surprisingly, J. William Fulbright, chairman of the Senate Foreign Relations Committee, supported Russell. It was surprising because Fulbright had opposed the Bay of Pigs landings and, a year earlier, in June, 1961, had noted the possibility that Soviet missiles would someday appear in Cuba and had said that he doubted that they would alter the balance of power in the world. It seemed to Fulbright that intercepting Soviet ships at sea was just as risky as taking out the bases themselves.

The president listened politely, but as he left the room he was heard to mutter under his breath something to the effect that if any of those so-and-sos wanted this job of his, they could have it.

SIX P.M.—DOBRYNIN TO SEE RUSK

Ambassador Dobrynin was in New York seeing Gromyko off when the State Department reached him to set up the six o'clock appointment. He flew back to Washington and going into Rusk's office he seemed relaxed. Twenty-five minutes later he came out clutching a copy of the president's speech in his hand—tense and, it seemed to reporters, shaken. "Ask the secretary," was the only reply he would give to questions.

SEVEN P.M.—THE PRESIDENT'S SPEECH

The president spoke to the nation and the world from his study. He began by describing U.S. surveillance and what it had discovered. He then pointed out the meaning of the missiles in Cuba. "This urgent transformation of Cuba into an important strategic base— by the presence of these large, long-range, and clearly offensive weapons of sudden mass destruction—constitutes an explicit threat to the peace and security of all the Americas."

He talked about the necessity for new standards of international conduct on a small planet in a nuclear age. "Nuclear weapons are so destructive and ballistic missiles so swift that any substantially increased possibility of their use or any sudden change in their deployment may well be regarded as a definite threat to peace."

The president went on to point out that for many years both the Soviet Union and the United States had recognized this fact and had deployed strategic nuclear weapons with great care, never upsetting the precarious status quo, which ensured that they would not be used in the absence of some vital challenge:

> Our own strategic missiles have never been transferred to the territory of any other nation under a cloak of secrecy and deception . . . this secret, swift, and extraordinary build-up of Communist missiles—in an area well known to have a special and historical relationship to the United States and the nations of the Western Hemisphere, in violation of Soviet assurances, and in defiance of American and hemispheric policy—this sudden, clandestine decision to station strategic weapons for the first time outside of Soviet soil—is a deliberately provocative and unjustified change in the status quo which cannot be accepted by this country if our courage and our commitments are ever to be trusted again by either friend or foe.

Finally, the president described what the United States intended to do about it:

> *First:* . . . a strict quarantine on all offensive military equipment under shipment to Cuba . . .
> *Second:* continued and increased close surveillance of Cuba . . . ,
> *Third:* It shall be the policy of this nation to regard any nuclear missile launched from Cuba against any nation in the Western Hemisphere as an attack by the Soviet Union on the United States, requiring a full retaliatory response upon the Soviet Union.
> *Fourth:* As a necessary military precaution I have reinforced our base at Guantánamo. . . .
> *Fifth:* We are calling tonight for an immediate meeting of the Organ of Consultation, under the Organization of American States, to consider this threat to hemispheric security and to invoke articles six and eight of the Rio Treaty in support of all necessary action. . . .
> *Sixth:* Under the Charter of the United Nations we are asking tonight that an emergency meeting of the Security Council be convoked without delay to take action against this latest Soviet threat to world peace. . . .

The world was witnessing its first crisis of the nuclear age, and the reaction was remarkable. It some parts of the United States, people stocked up on canned goods and dug bomb shelters. Some city dwellers evacuated to the countryside. But most people in the United States and in all the other countries of the world recognized the futility of individual action and watched with breathless fascination the duel between the two greatest military powers of the world and the two lonely men who headed them.

The first Soviet reaction was a long propaganda statement, accusing the United States of violating international law, of provocative acts, of "piracy," and a vehement denial that the arms they were sending to Cuba were intended for anything but defensive purposes. The statement seemed designed to stall until the Soviets had time to decide on their next move.

The Latin American reaction was crucial. The Organization of American States met on Tuesday and approved the proposed American resolution overwhelmingly—19 to 0—partly due to the hard and brilliant work of Assistant Secretary Edwin M. Martin and partly due to the courage of Latin American leaders who defied their leftist opposition and of such men as Emilio Sarmiento Carruncho of Bolivia, who could not get through to his government for instructions but who at the risk of his political life still voted yes.

There was also in Kennedy's speech an attempt, in the words of Abram Chayes, the State Department's legal adviser, "to make a little international law for the nuclear age." The speech took the position that "[n]uclear weapons are so destructive and ballistic missiles so swift that any substantially increased possibility of their use or any sudden change in their deployment may well be regarded as a definite threat to peace."

The best of both worlds was not only to make such a contribution to international law, but also to have an airtight case in the context of the earlier treaty provisions and procedures of the OAS, which rested on the legitimacy of collective action by a regional organization, qualifying under Chapter VIII of the UN Charter. This is what the overwhelming endorsement of the OAS accomplished. What it also accomplished was a massive demonstration to Moscow of inter-American solidarity.

Prompt support also came from our NATO Allies. At first there had been some doubts expressed in the British press that there really were Soviet missiles in Cuba. But then President Kennedy authorized the release of the pictures, and all doubts were swept aside. (The same thing had happened when Rusk and I had briefed the ambassadors from the "unaligned" states and showed them the pictures. Many had stopped as they left the hall to wish the United States luck in the confrontation ahead.) Dean Acheson briefed General de Gaulle, Chancellor Adenauer, and the NATO Council, and all of the NATO governments gave their support.

At the UN, the United States called for a meeting of the Security Council, and on Thursday Ambassador Adlai E. Stevenson presented the American case. He ended his speech by confronting the Soviet ambassador, Valerian A. Zorin. "All right, sir," Stevenson said, "let me ask you one simple question. Do you, Ambassador Zorin, deny that the USSR has placed and is placing medium—and intermediate—range missiles and sites in Cuba? Yes or no—don't wait for the translation—yes or no?"

"I am not standing in the dock of an American court and I shall not answer at this stage," was Zorin's reply.

"I am prepared to wait for my answer until hell freezes over, if that is your decision," Ambassador Stevenson said, "and I am also prepared to present the evidence in this room."

And he turned to the enlargements of the U–2 photographs, convincing the world of Soviet guilt and mustering support for the action the United States was about to take.

NOTE

1. *New York Times,* August 28, 1987, pp. 1, 9.

Chapter 7

The Resolution

To avoid forcing the Soviet Union into a corner that might lead to what Kennedy called a "spasm reaction," he and his advisers had crafted a gradual, step-by-step policy that would give the Soviets plenty of time to ponder the consequences of their response to each move by the United States.

Twenty-four hours passed before the OAS could meet and approve the proposal for a quarantine, a delay that Kennedy wanted and planned for.

Having obtained the OAS approval, Kennedy then announced that the quarantine would go into effect on Wednesday, October 24, at 10:00 a.m.—providing still another 24-hour pause.

He then instructed the Navy to wait another 24 hours before stopping a Soviet ship—still another pause.

What is more, Kennedy deliberately chose as the first ship to be stopped a Soviet oil tanker, the *Bucharest*—precisely because it could not possibly carry any arms. The *Bucharest* was hailed on Thursday, October 25, but not boarded. Still another 24 hours passed.

The first boarding did not occur until Friday, October 26, at 8:00 a.m.—and Kennedy had ordered that the ship to be boarded should *not* be a Soviet ship. So the choice was a Lebanese freighter on Soviet charter, which would clearly *not* be carrying any sensitive armaments.

Two days earlier, on Wednesday, October 24, the President had authorized the Navy to fly low-level reconnaissance flights over the missile sites, and the pictures revealed that work was proceeding at a frantic speed.

These pictures also revealed for the first time the presence of Soviet ground forces. During the crisis, American intelligence estimated the number of troops to be about 20,000. Some years later the United States learned that they actually numbered 42,000.

What was a surprise at the time—an extremely alarming surprise—was that the first of the low-level photos showed 6 launchers for battlefield nuclear missiles with a range of about 40 kilometers. These were the ground-to-ground battlefield nuclear missiles that the Soviets called the Luna and American intelligence had dubbed the Frog. Subsequent flights identified another 8 such launchers, making a total of 14.

The photos did not pick up any warheads for any of the missiles, whether medium-range, intermediate-range, or battlefield. But this was to be expected, since the warheads were small and easily concealed. However, American intelligence assumed that in the case of the battlefield nuclear weapons, the warheads would actually accompany the launchers.

The reasoning behind this conclusion was as follows. The obvious purpose of these missiles was to protect the MRBMs and IRBMs from ground attacks from the American base at Guantánamo and from American invasion forces coming from the sea. The Soviets would naturally expect that an invasion, if it came, would be preceded by extremely heavy air bombardment which might severely damage the ability of the local Soviet commanders to communicate with Moscow. So it was only logical that the Soviets would decide in advance that the Lunas would have to have their warheads with them. For these same reasons, it was also only logical that the Soviets would decide to give the local commander the authority to fire the Lunas if an invasion actually occurred and if communications were cut off—*without further checking with Moscow.*[1]

Because the American Army expected to be met with battlefield nuclear weapons, its contingency plan for a possible invasion also called for tactical nuclear weapons—the nuclear-capable eight-inch howitzer, the Honest John nuclear rocket, and the very short range nuclear mortar, the Davy Crockett. McGeorge Bundy later wrote that he did not realize at the time that the Army planned to include battlefield nuclear weapons in their equipment and that if an invasion had actually been ordered, he was confident that Kennedy, McNamara, or Maxwell Taylor would have made sure that the tactical nuclear weapons were left behind. I have no doubt at all that the Army would have been ordered to keep any tactical nuclear weapons well to the rear and that they would not have been permitted to use them unless President Kennedy gave his express permission. I also have no doubt that Kennedy would have given that permission only if the Soviets had used their battlefield nuclear weapons first. But since we knew the Soviet troops defending the missiles were armed with battlefield nuclear weapons it would have been unduly risky not to give the American forces the same capability.

Also on Wednesday, the Soviets rejected the U.S. quarantine proclamation. Ominously, the Soviet ships heading for Cuba were joined by six Soviet submarines.

As already mentioned, neither the U–2 nor the low-level reconnaissance planes had taken pictures of anything that looked like a warhead. However, some of the structures the Soviets were building at the missile sites were clearly intended to house the warheads. For safety reasons such buildings had to have very thick walls and very thin roofs so that an accidental nuclear explosion would be directed into the upper atmosphere rather than the immediate surroundings. These buildings were never completed.

Also, to send warheads by ship would have risked their being captured and the secrets of their construction revealed. Although not ruling out the possibility that the warheads would come by ship along with the missiles themselves, the American officials concerned decided that for these two reasons the more likely possibility was that the warheads would be sent by air. Accordingly, the United States asked the African states on the route to Cuba to deny Soviet aircraft landing and refueling rights. They readily agreed. As a consequence, the Soviet planes bringing the warheads might well have had to be refueled in the air. The United States carefully monitored the skies for evidence that this was being done and found none.

However, when the crisis was in full swing a very large jet aircraft

departed from Moscow and headed for Cuba. An emergency meeting at the White House speculated that this airplane, equipped with
large fuel tanks for long flights, might be the one carrying the warheads. Robert Kennedy and others thought that the United States
had no choice but to shoot the plane down over the Atlantic. Finally,
however, it was decided to let the plane land, but to keep it under
air surveillance with fighter-bombers standing by, and if warheads
started coming out of the airplane's hold to attack immediately and
destroy them on the ground. As it turned out, the plane was inau-
gurating a new Aeroflot route to Cuba, and its cargo consisted of
about 200 journalists!

In October, 1992, the CIA held a public conference on the thir-
tieth anniversary of the missile crisis. The photointerpreters present
confirmed that two weeks after the crisis was over, photo reconnaissance showed some vans with a very peculiar shape being
brought out from the cover of some woods at Mariel—which was
about 100 kilometers from the missile sites—and being loaded onto
the first ship back to the Soviet Union, the *Alexandrov*. Why should
these peculiarly shaped vans have such a very high priority? Photos
of MRBM sites in the Soviet Union were reexamined, and these same
peculiarly shaped vans were found to be present. This left no doubt
that these vans were carrying the MRBM warheads we had never
seen.[2]

Then, late on Wednesday, October 24, came the first hint of a
break—some of the Soviet ships heading toward Cuba altered
course. These included ships with extra-large hatches that the United
States suspected were the ones that were being used to carry the 60-
foot-long missiles. The rest of the ships stopped dead in the water,
wallowing while they waited for orders.

Secretary of State Rusk, recalling a boyhood game in which the
two opponents tried to stare each other down "eyeball to eyeball,"
remarked that "the other fellow just blinked."

As it turned out, this was not really a blink. At best it was only
a sign that the Soviets realized what President Kennedy had been
stressing all along to the ExCom—that in a nuclear confrontation
neither side could afford to take precipitate action. A scribbled sign
chalked on the blackboard of the briefing room of the State Department's Bureau of Intelligence and Research made the same point
with gallows humor: "In a Nuclear Age," it read, "nations must

make war as porcupines make love—carefully." By stopping the ships, the Soviets were probably only being careful.

The American Navy had a more sinister interpretation. They suspected that the ships had altered course in order to pick up more Soviet submarines as escorts.

The president was determined to pace events, and issued orders that there was to be no shooting. The Soviet ships were to be kept in view but none was to be boarded until President Kennedy issued the instructions.

Although the Navy objected, Kennedy wanted the interception line to be drawn close in to Cuba—so that Khrushchev would have plenty of time for thought—instead of at a distance, where the Navy traditionally drew blockade lines. This led to a bitter clash between McNamara and Admiral George W. Anderson, the chief of naval operations. McNamara went to the Navy Flag Plot, the Navy's command center, and began to question Anderson sharply and in detail—asking who would make the first interception, whether Russian-speaking officers were on board the intercepting ships, and so on. Admiral Anderson apparently felt that Secretary McNamara's questioning constituted undue interference in the details of the Navy's work. McNamara, on the other hand, felt that he had a responsibility to make sure that the details of execution did not upset the president's carefully planned strategy.

Later it transpired that the Navy did *not* draw the interception line close in to shore, as the president had directed in order to give Khrushchev as much time as possible to consider the Soviet response, but well out to sea in accordance with Navy tradition.

It also later transpired that the Navy made it a practice during the crisis to maneuver in such a way that the Soviet submarines would have to surface to recharge their batteries in the presence of the American warships. In fact, in some cases the American ships used practice depth charges to drive the Soviet submarines to the surface.

On Friday, October 26, low-level reconnaissance flights showed that work on the missile sites was still proceeding at a furious pace. A White House announcement describing these activities concluded that the Soviets were trying to achieve "full operational capability as soon as possible." No one on the American side could forget the portentous implications if the Soviets got the MRBMs fully operational. The MRBMs would be able to destroy half the cities in the United States. And when the IRBMs became operational, they would be able to destroy all the rest with the sole exception of Seattle.

Throughout Friday, the president communicated the American sense of urgency in a number of ways. He emphasized it in his message to U Thant, the secretary-general of the United Nations. He had executive branch officials repeat it in their conversations at the UN, with the press, and with congressional leaders. On Friday, the general feeling in Washington—which was communicated to the Soviets—was that the United States could hold off its next move for no more than one or two days.

THE FIRST REAL BLINK

But this was the day of the first real blink.

There were five basic channels of communication between the Soviet and American governments. One was by formal letter between the heads of government using embassy facilities. The mechanism was for the Soviets, for example, to deliver a letter from Khrushchev for Kennedy to the American embassy in Moscow. The embassy would translate the letter into English and cable it to Washington. Usually, but not always, the Soviets would also cable the letter to their embassy in Washington, who delivered a copy to the State Department.

Second, the Soviets—characteristically—maintained alternative sets of channels that bypassed their embassy in Washington and probably were handled in special ways at the Moscow end as well.

Third, views could be exchanged formally and officially by note or by letters between officials of lesser rank than the heads of government.

Fourth, there could be an informal but still official exchange— orally, for example—between the Soviet ambassador and an official in the State Department or the White House.

Finally, the Soviets not infrequently used entirely unofficial channels. A special officer with a nominal title as a working-level official or a Tass correspondent with unusual connections might be used to push a line or communicate a threat. Occasionally, the Soviets might use such an unofficial channel to try out a proposal or test a reaction in advance and so avoid committing themselves prematurely.

In the Cuban missile crisis, all five channels were used—several formal letters were exchanged between Kennedy and Khrushchev; there were several less formal exchanges, as, for example, between Attorney General Robert F. Kennedy and Ambassador Dobrynin; and there were several entirely unofficial conversations, such as hints dropped by Tass correspondents at the UN. But the decisive channels were probably the letters between Kennedy and Khrushchev, the exchanges between Robert Kennedy and Ambassador Dobrynin, and one very unusual channel of the last type, the very informal and unofficial. It was over such an unofficial channel that the first hint of a real blink came in.

Aleksander Fomin, whom the Americans knew to be head of the Washington office of the KGB, sought out John Scali, an ABC correspondent. The Soviets knew that Scali and I were friends, and Fomin asked Scali if he could find out from me if the highest levels of the U.S. government would be interested in the following solution to the crisis:

1. The Soviets would withdraw the missiles in Cuba.

2. UN inspectors would be allowed to supervise and verify the removal.

3. The Soviet Union would promise not to reintroduce missiles to Cuba—*ever*.

4. The United States would pledge publicly not to invade Cuba.

Scali told Fomin that if the message was genuine and if it had indeed originated at the highest levels of the Soviet government, then he believed that I, as the head of the State Department's intelligence bureau, would be willing to convey it to the secretary of state and the president. Fomin repeatedly assured Scali that the message came from Khrushchev himself. Scali took it to me, and after hearing of Fomin's assurances that the message came from Khrushchev himself, I took it to Rusk and Kennedy.

The president and the secretary, after discussing the matter with other members of the ExCom, decided the Fomin approach was worth pursuing. Rusk asked me to bring Scali to his office by way of the secretary's private elevator. In his office, Rusk asked Scali to go back to Fomin and tell him the United States was interested, but that time was very, very short—no more than two days. Rusk had written what Scali was to say on a piece of yellow paper in his own handwriting:

> I have reason to believe that the USG [United States Government] sees real possibilities and supposes that the representatives of the two governments in New York could work this matter out with U Thant and with each other. My impression is, however, that time is very urgent.

THE CABLE FROM KHRUSHCHEV

That evening a long, rambling "four-part" cable—a letter from Khrushchev to Kennedy—began to come in. Unaccountably, it took 10 hours to arrive in Washington.[3] The message was conciliatory, but it contained nothing specific. One key passage, for example, likened the crisis to two men pulling on each end of a rope with a knot in the middle:

> Mr. President, we ought not to pull on the ends of the rope in which you have tied the knot of war because the more the two of us pull, the tighter that knot will be tied, and the moment may come when it will be tied so tight that we will not have the strength to untie it and then it will be necessary to cut the knot, to doom the world to the catastrophe of nuclear war.

The Soviets had on earlier occasions used this technique of sending a vague message through official channels and a very specific message through unofficial, easily deniable channels. The combination of the approach through Fomin and the long cable from Khrushchev convinced most of us that this was the break that we had all been hoping for. The cable communicated a willingness to negotiate but gave no specifics; the Fomin message gave the specifics.[4]

At Secretary Rusk's request several of us in the Bureau of Intelligence and Research (INR) spent the whole night analyzing the two messages—"to include" as Rusk said, "any hookers in it"—to be ready for the president and the members of the ExCom when they met the next morning.

As we pored over the rambling Khrushchev cable, it became even more clear to us that Fomin's approach through Scali and the Khrushchev cable were really a single package. We even felt we could visualize the circumstances in which the decision was taken and the messages written. We pictured the Politburo in continuous session for several hours with Khrushchev in the chair. A decision is reached to offer an olive branch through the double approach—a vague but encouraging cable from Khrushchev and an unofficial approach through Fomin that offered specifics. Khrushchev calls in a secretary and dictates the cable. Long, rambling, and wordy, the cable seemed to us to be pure Khrushchev.

Many years later, high Soviet officials confirmed that our speculations about the circumstances—the Politburo meeting and Khrushchev himself dictating the cable—were in fact correct.

In any case, our judgment was that the Soviets had indeed blinked and that even though there were some possible hookers to be guarded against, the proposals should be taken very seriously.

It was apparently Fomin's assignment to stimulate the U.S. government's interest in Khrushchev's imprecise formulations by adding specifics—especially on the question of inspection, which Moscow knew was central for the United States. There were hints of other important points scattered through the Khrushchev cable like "raisins in a cake," as George Ball aptly put it, but the all-important offer of inspection had not appeared at all.

From all the evidence, it seemed to us that Khrushchev had faced the prospect of an escalating confrontation squarely, that he was horrified at what he saw at the end of that road, and that he was sincerely searching for a way out. On the other hand, there was still the possibility that he was only playing for time until the missiles were fully operational. The missile experts calculated that this would happen in the last days of October in the case of the MRBMs and about mid-November for the IRBMs, which had not yet arrived. So the members of the ExCom agreed that a precondition for further negotiations should be that the Soviets stop work on the missile sites.

When the ExCom met at ten o'clock on Saturday morning hopes were running high. Then, at 10:17 a.m., the news tickers cleared the first bulletin of a new statement being broadcast by Radio Moscow. As the details came in it seemed clear that the Soviets had reversed their position. What they offered now was to trade their missiles in Cuba for American missiles in Turkey.

News also came in that a single Soviet ship had detached itself from the others outside the quarantine line and was steaming straight for Cuba. It looked very much as if the Soviets had decided to test our determination in a confrontation at sea after all—or even to provoke an incident.

Worse news quickly followed. The SAM network of antiaircraft missiles had become operational. An American U–2 had been shot down, and the pilot, Major Rudolf Anderson, Jr., had been killed.

The ExCom was also informed that the CIA had concluded that 24 of the MRBMs were fully operational.[5] It also had to be assumed that the 44 operational ICBMs based inside the Soviet Union had been placed on alert. For its part, the United States had 140 ICBMs aimed at the Soviet Union on alert and about 200 bombers armed with H-bombs on continuous airborne alert.

It was the blackest hour of the crisis. The ExCom had already considered what the American response should be if a U–2 was shot down. The decision had been that the one antiaircraft SAM site responsible should be taken out immediately in a bombing attack and that if a second U–2 was shot down *all* the SAM sites on the island should be taken out.

In any case, Washington reasoned, the Soviets must have realized that shooting down U–2s would force the United States to take direct action against the SAMs, and shooting down the U–2 therefore seemed to mean that they had decided on a showdown.

There was speculation that the hard-liners in the Kremlin might be taking over, possibly backed by the military. Another speculation was that some of the people meeting around the equivalent table in the Kremlin thought they could extract a higher price.

It seemed obvious that the Moscow broadcast linking the Soviet missiles in Cuba to the American Jupiter missiles in Turkey had been inspired by a newspaper column published on Wednesday by Walter Lippmann proposing that missiles in Turkey be traded for missiles in Cuba. The hard-liners may have pushed the other members of the Soviet leadership to force Kennedy to equate the two, which would tend to justify the Soviet decision to deploy missiles to Cuba in the eyes of the rest of the world, who did not know that Kennedy had long before made a decision to remove the American missiles from Turkey.

But none of this really accounted for either the shoot-down of the U–2 or the fact that a Soviet ship was now speeding for the interception line. If the Soviets were bargaining, it was a highly dangerous way to do it. It simply would not be possible in these circumstances to keep the pace of events from escalating. Everything would be foreshortened, and an actual invasion of Cuba might be no later than 48 hours away.

THE "STRANGELOVE" INCIDENT[6]

Then it was the American turn to make a slip. Early that afternoon as a small meeting in his office with Ambassador Thompson was breaking up, Rusk drafted me to carry a proposed response to the Moscow broadcast over to the White House, where I was going for another purpose anyway. When I arrived, the president and McGeorge Bundy were talking in the little office occupied by Mrs. Lincoln, the president's secretary. After a short discussion about the proposed message during which the president indicated that he preferred to wait until the ExCom met that afternoon, I left to return to the State Department.

As I passed the ground-floor entrance by McGeorge Bundy's office, one of Bundy's aides grabbed me to say that my office was calling me—urgently.

The caller was Joseph Scott, a deputy director of INR whose responsibilities included coordinating U–2 operations worldwide. He said that in his other hand he had a phone connected to the war room of the Pentagon. Another U–2—totally unrelated to the missile crisis—on a routine air-sampling mission from Alaska to the North Pole had picked the wrong star for its return flight and was at that moment over the Soviet Union. Soviet fighter planes had scrambled. The U–2 pilot had gone on the air—in the clear—calling frantically for help. American fighters in Alaska had also scrambled and were attempting to rendezvous with the U–2 to escort it home.

I ran upstairs and found the president and Bundy still in Mrs. Lincoln's office. The president knew at a glance that something was terribly wrong. Out of breath from running upstairs and pale and shaky from over 30 hours without sleep, I told my story.

The implications were as obvious as they were horrendous. The Soviets might well regard this U–2 flight as a last-minute intelligence reconnaissance in preparation for nuclear war. It was just this sort of invitation to miscalculation that Kennedy's detailed instructions had been designed to prevent. "One of your planes," Khrushchev himself later wrote, "violates our frontier during this anxious time we are both experiencing, when everything has been put into combat readiness. Is it not a fact that an intruding American plane could easily be taken for a nuclear bomber, which might push us to a fateful step . . . ?"

Ernest Hemingway once described true courage as "grace under pressure." The president was the first to break the awestruck silence. He gave a short, ironic laugh. "There is always some son of a bitch," he said, "who doesn't get the word."[7]

THE KHRUSHCHEV CABLE AND THE MOSCOW BROADCAST COMPARED

Although he was well aware of the reasons for the delay in removing the Jupiters from Turkey, the president was annoyed to think that in spite of his earlier instructions to remove them, they were still there, political albatrosses around his neck. The missiles in Turkey were obsolete, and removing them would not be any great problem in subsequent negotiations. But that did not help now. The immediate threat was that the Soviets were continuing construction of the missile bases at a rapid pace. There could be no negotiations while that rapid buildup continued. A statement was quickly drafted as a response to the Soviet proposal and released as a public statement. It suggested that the missiles in Turkey would be no problem in subsequent negotiations but that such negotiations could not take place while work continued on the Soviet bases in Cuba.

At the same time, before I went home to bed, both I and the group in INR who had spent the night analyzing Khrushchev's cable and Fomin's message took a hard look at the broadcast from Moscow linking the Soviet missiles in Cuba with the U.S. missiles in Turkey. What leaped out of the page was that while the Khrushchev cable was pure Khrushchev, the Moscow broadcast was pure Soviet bureaucratese. It seemed almost a certainty that the Moscow broadcast had been drafted on Wednesday, October 24, as a propaganda ploy picking up on Walter Lippmann's presumptuous and irresponsible column linking the missiles in Turkey to those in Cuba.[8] We calculated that the statement had been circulating through the Soviet government for clearances on Thursday and Friday, and broadcast Saturday morning. It was a typical case of the bureaucratic left hand of a government not knowing that the leadership right hand had developed an entirely different policy.

We quickly had a memo hand-carried to the president and the other members of the ExCom spelling out our conclusions:

1. The Khrushchev cable and the Fomin approach had been developed *after* the Moscow broadcast had been drafted, not before.

2. The broadcast had all the earmarks of a low-level, bureaucratic initiative to take advantage of Lippmann's piece.

3. The two-pronged approach of a forthcoming but general cable from Khrushchev and a behind-the-scenes but specific proposal through Fomin had been developed at the very highest level of the Soviet government.

Also about the same time, the Navy reported that the Soviet ship headed toward Cuba was an oil tanker, and so could not be carrying any war materiel. President Kennedy ordered the Navy to let it pass.

Kennedy also decided to postpone for at least a day or two the retaliatory bombing of the SAM site that the ExCom had previously concluded was the appropriate response if a U–2 was shot down. Before retaliating, Kennedy wanted first to craft a message to Khrushchev and, second, to wait for Khrushchev's reply.

But some way still had to be found to get back to the more promising proposals put forward on Friday—and quickly.

Rusk called Scali to his office later that Saturday afternoon and suggested he see Fomin again and ask what had happened. Had the whole operation been a trap to divert attention while the Soviets planned a double cross? What was going on in the Kremlin?

When Scali and Fomin met, Fomin seemed puzzled and unhappy. He sought to explain the morning's broadcast from Moscow linking the missiles in Cuba to those in Turkey and reneging on his formula of the night before as being the result of bad communications. He speculated that the Saturday morning cable had been drafted before his report on the favorable American reaction had arrived.

Exploding, Scali accused Fomin of a double cross. After Scali calmed down, Fomin assured him that a reply would surely come soon, and Scali repeated that time was very short. Scali went straight to the State Department to report.

THE "TROLLOPE PLOY"

With all the evidence on the table, the ExCom met to consider what to do next. And it was Robert Kennedy who conceived a brilliant diplomatic maneuver—later dubbed the "Trollope ploy" after the recurrent scene in Anthony Trollope's novels in which the girl interprets a squeeze of her hand as a proposal of marriage.[9]

Robert Kennedy's suggestion was to deal only with Friday's package of signals—Khrushchev's cable and the Fomin approach—as if the conflicting Moscow broadcast on Saturday linking the missiles in Cuba with those in Turkey simply did not exist. The Moscow broadcast, as already mentioned, had in fact already been rejected in a public announcement. The thing to do now, Robert Kennedy suggested, was to answer the Friday package of approaches and make the answer public—which would add a certain political pressure as well as increase the speed.

Khrushchev's Friday night cable had not mentioned or even hinted at inspection, but inspection had been a key element in the proposal put forward by Fomin. Selecting welcome points like this from the Fomin approach and others from the Khrushchev cable, the ExCom drafted a statement for the president's signature:

I have read your letter of October 26th with great care and welcome the statement of your desire to seek a prompt solution to the problem. The first thing that needs to be done, however, is for work to cease on offensive missile bases in Cuba. . . . Assuming this is done promptly, I have given my representatives in New York instructions that will permit them to work out this weekend—in cooperation with the Acting Secretary General and your representative—an arrangement for the permanent solution to the Cuban problem.

Then came the "Trollope ploy":

As I read your letter, the key elements of your proposals—which seem generally acceptable as I understand them—are as follows: (1) You would agree to remove the weapons systems from Cuba under appropriate UN observation and supervision [which had been mentioned only by Fomin]; and undertake, with suitable safeguards, to halt the further introduction of such weapons systems into Cuba. (2) We, on our part, would agree—upon establishment of adequate arrangements through the United Nations to ensure the carrying out and continuation of these commitments—(a) to remove promptly the quarantine measures now in effect and (b) to give assurances against an invasion of Cuba.

This message was released for broadcast to Moscow and the public.

The president then personally dispatched Robert Kennedy to talk to Dobrynin. At Rusk's suggestion, Robert Kennedy was first to explain to Dobrynin that while there could be no *deal* linking the missiles in Cuba and those in Turkey, President Kennedy himself had been determined for some time to have the missiles in Turkey removed. The United States did not have the authority to make the decision without the concurrence of NATO, but the United States would undertake to get that concurrence as soon as the crisis was over—so long as Moscow did not try to claim that removing the missiles from Turkey was part of a bargain.

Khrushchev says in his memoirs that President Kennedy said that in exchange for the Soviets removing missiles from Cuba the United States would remove missiles from Turkey and Italy (the U.K. had already announced before the crisis began that the Thors were being removed). "We knew perfectly well," Khrushchev wrote, "that this pledge was of a symbolic nature: the American rockets in Turkey and Italy were already obsolete, and the Americans would promptly replace them with more modern ones. Besides, the US was already equipping its navy with Polaris missiles. Nevertheless, by agreeing even to symbolic measures, Kennedy was creating the impression of mutual concessions."[10]

One assumes that by this latter statement Khrushchev meant that the impression of mutual concessions made his task of dealing with his colleagues and the Soviet military easier.

The president had wanted the Jupiters out of Turkey from the beginning of his administration, and he was annoyed that they were still there. But everyone concerned feared that if there was a public trade the effects on our NATO Allies would be very bad. Inevitably, many Europeans would see it as selling out a small Ally in the face of Soviet pressure. Confidence in the American nuclear umbrella over Europe would be shaken to its foundations.

Fearful of the effects that even a promise to remove the Jupiters from Turkey might have on the NATO countries—even though they all knew that Kennedy had all along intended to remove them—the members of the ExCom agreed that the promise should be kept secret. And Robert Kennedy was instructed to tell Dobrynin that the Soviets must observe the same secrecy or the promise would be null and void. It was not until 1969, the year after Robert Kennedy's death, when his book *Thirteen Days* was published, that the promise became public.

The Jupiters in Turkey were obsolete, while the Soviet missiles in Cuba were both more modern and more effective—"highly reliable, accurate, and powerful" is how one specialist described them.[11] Because of this disparity in the two missile systems, it is highly unlikely that the Soviets would have accepted a trade without the pressure of the quarantine.

In the first place, the Soviets undoubtedly understood that the missiles in Cuba would not be covered by the existing American warning system. General Thomas Power, the SAC commander, said emphatically that the missiles "could have hit us with virtually no warning" and could "virtually wipe out our entire nuclear strike capability within a span of thirty minutes."[12]

Second, without a blockade the 40 missile pads in Cuba would probably have been only the first of several more missile deployments. Without a quarantine the Soviets could, in the words of Raymond Garthoff, an authority on the Soviet military and at the time of the crisis a staff member of the State Department's Office of Politico-Military Affairs, "literally multiply the number of launchers to a force large enough to threaten the entire strategic balance of power."[13]

In addition to all these military consequences of permitting the missiles to remain in Cuba, President Kennedy was also sensitive to the political consequences. The political damage to the United States of permitting even one Soviet missile to remain in Cuba would have been severe—as Kennedy said, "It would have politically changed the balance of power." He was convinced that if the missiles did not come out, "no one would be able to conduct a sensible American foreign policy for years to come."[14]

In addition to explaining to Dobrynin President Kennedy's feelings about the Jupiters, Robert Kennedy was to make crystal clear to him the full sense of urgency and seriousness felt in Washington, the fact that the United States could wait no longer but would have to proceed immediately to the next step—toward an agreement and peace if the missiles were withdrawn from Cuba, or, if they were not, toward "strong and overwhelming retaliatory action." What the United States could not do, the attorney general made clear, was to remain any longer on dead center.

Now there was nothing to do but wait. As the meeting broke up, President Kennedy remarked that it could "go either way."

Just before nine o'clock Sunday morning, October 28, Moscow Radio announced that it would have an important statement to broadcast at nine sharp. It was a letter from Chairman Khrushchev:

> In order to eliminate as rapidly as possible the conflict which endangers the cause of peace . . . the Soviet Government . . . has given a new order to dismantle the arms which you described as offensive, and to crate and return them to the Soviet Union.

To tie the final strings, a White House statement was quickly drafted confirming the agreement and just as quickly broadcast over the Voice of America. A fuller reply to the chairman's letter was then prepared and this, too, was released for publication and broadcast.[15]

The crisis was over. The two greatest military powers in the world had avoided war—nuclear war—and the tension subsided.

No one knows for sure what Khrushchev felt, but there are a few clues. In a speech in December reporting on the crisis, he spoke of "a smell of burning in the air," indicating that he felt the world had come close indeed to a nuclear holocaust and that his own personal feeling was a sense of relief.[16]

Another hint of how Khrushchev felt came the same Sunday that the crisis ended. Late that day, October 28, Scali met with Fomin for the last time. "I have been instructed," Fomin said in the classic language of diplomacy, "to thank you and to tell you that the information you supplied was very valuable to the chairman in helping him make up his mind quickly. And," he added with a smile, "that includes your 'explosion' Saturday."

As for Kennedy, he was naturally elated. But he permitted himself to express it only privately, to his brother Robert, and he did so with his typical wryness: "Maybe this is the night I should go to the theater"—thinking of Abraham Lincoln and the theater known as Ford's.

NOTES

1. In the discussions later held between Soviets and Americans about the crisis, described below, the Soviet participants confirmed that the warheads did accompany the Lunas and that the local Soviet commander did have the authority to fire them if there was an invasion and *if communications with Moscow had been cut off.*

2. When castigated for not passing this information on to those of us in the White House and the State Department at the time, the CIA representatives at the conference responded that since the crisis was over when the discovery was made they did not want to bother us! Ray S. Cline, who at the time of the crisis was the CIA's deputy director for intelligence, wrote in an article in *Foreign Affairs* published 27 years after the crisis that he did not believe that the warheads ever arrived in Cuba (Fall, 1989, pp. 191–92). Either Cline's memory had failed spectacularly or the photointerpreters decided not to bother the top levels of the CIA as well!

3. This delay became a major factor in the postcrisis decision by the United States and the Soviet Union to establish a 24-hours-a-day, 365-days-a-year "hot line" between the White House and the Kremlin.

4. At about the same time that Fomin was speaking to Scali, U Thant made what was a strikingly similar proposal for defusing the crisis to Adlai Stevenson. The way that U Thant presented the proposal made everyone believe that the idea was his own, so there was no clear or promising way to follow through on it. However, several years later U Thant revealed to Dean Rusk that the idea had come from a Soviet official whom we all knew to be, like Fomin, a high official in the KGB. U Thant also insisted that Gromyko had known about the approach. As Rusk said when he recalled U Thant's conversation, "That would have been very different, had we known that." The fact that the same message was being peddled by another KGB agent would have removed all doubt that the approach was coming from Khrushchev. However, since we decided to treat the Fomin message as genuine, no harm was done.

5. In the conference between Americans, Soviets, and Cubans on the crisis held in Havana in 1992, a Soviet general said that at this time some of the MRBM warheads were still enroute but that 36 had already arrived in Cuba.

6. So named by the American participants in the crisis after the movie *Dr. Strangelove, or How I Learned to Stop Worrying and Love the Bomb*. In this movie the world was destroyed in a nuclear war caused when a single American bomber, whose radio had been knocked out by antiaircraft fire, did not get the message to turn back, and dropped a nuclear bomb on the Soviet Union. The bomb's explosion in turn set off a "doomsday" machine of nuclear missiles that was triggered automatically by a nuclear explosion anywhere in the world.

In real life, the Soviet Union's "doomsday" machine was not developed until the 1970s, but it is still operational in the Russia of today (see Bruce G. Blair, "Russia's Doomsday Machine," *New York Times,* October 8, 1993, p. A35). To guarantee retaliation even if Moscow and the civilian and military leadership has been annihilated, the system would be activated in the early stages of a crisis by a "fail deadly" message from the general staff's underground war room in Moscow to a distant radio bunker at Chekov. The message would contain components of the "unlock" codes that prevent unauthorized launches. A small team at the radio bunker is all that is needed to activate the whole system—the rest is fully automated. When electronic devices show both a breakdown of communications to headquarters in Moscow and the presence of nuclear explosions, the apparatus issues an order to launch, complete with unlock codes, and transmits it through buried, low-frequency antennae to another set of special complexes several hundred miles away.

At these complexes, communications rockets hidden in SS–17 silos and on mobile SS–25 launchers would automatically record the instructions and the unlock codes and automatically launch themselves on trajectories that traverse all the ICBM missile launching sites. As the communications rockets passed over ICBM complexes, they would issue the necessary orders and unlock codes. Both fixed and mobile ICBMs would be launched automatically, without any participation by local crews and completely bypassing local missile commanders.

7. The president told me to get on top of the situation imme-

diately, to ensure that the Soviets were informed that the U–2 intrusion was an accident totally unrelated to the crisis, and to make certain that our planes took care to avoid any provocation of any kind. I turned to carry out the instructions, but dizzy from lack of sleep, I would have fallen if McGeorge Bundy had not steadied me. He told the president that I had not been to bed for a couple of days and asked if someone else might not take care of the problem. The president looked at me keenly, ordered me to go home and get some sleep, and told Bundy to find someone else to handle the problem. The plane returned safely. The Soviets made no follow-up move, and the president decided to ignore the incident. Later, when Khrushchev made his protest, Kennedy apologized.

This U–2 incident, like the delay in the four-part message from Khrushchev, was important in bringing about the establishment of the so-called hot line providing around-the-clock communications between Moscow and Washington that was established after the crisis.

8. It was presumptuous of Lippmann to undertake to instruct the U.S. government when it had been working night and day on the crisis for 10 days. It was irresponsible of him to publish the piece in the midst of a crisis, when he did not know of Kennedy's effort to remove the Jupiters from Turkey and had made no attempt to check with the administration to find out its view of the missiles in Turkey and whether or not it had been trying to do something about them. The incident is an illustration of self-important journalism— or at least self-important columnist journalism—at its worst.

9. Shortly after the Moscow broadcast was received linking the missiles in Cuba with those in Turkey, Bundy suggested a reply saying that the United States "would prefer to deal with your interesting proposals of last night" rather than the trade proposed in the broadcast. What was original about Robert Kennedy's suggestion—and what made it a "Trollope ploy"—was the idea of having the reply to Khrushchev completely ignore the Saturday morning broadcast, which had already been answered by a public rejection, and pretend that nothing had been said on either side since the long cable from Khrushchev had been received the night before.

10. Strobe Talbot, translator and editor, *Khrushchev Remembers: The Last Testament* (Boston: Little, Brown, 1974), p. 512.

11. Raymond L. Garthoff, *Intelligence Assessment and Policy-*

making: A Decision Point in the Kennedy Administration (Washington, DC: The Brookings Institution, 1984), pp. 32–33.

12. General Thomas S. Power with Albert A. Arnhym, *Design for Survival* (New York: Coward-McCann, 1965), p. 154.

13. Raymond L. Garthoff, *Reflections on the Cuban Missile Crisis* (Washington, DC: The Brookings Institution, 1987), pp. 138–46.

14. McGeorge Bundy, *Danger and Survival: Choices about the Bomb in the First Fifty Years* (New York: Random House, 1988), p. 412.

15. Khrushchev's message made no mention of the American Jupiters in Turkey. Years later, Soviets who were aides to top officials at the time told me that the Soviet leaders saw that most people understood both the difference between a secret deployment and a public one and the fact that the American missiles in Turkey were outmoded and virtually useless while the Soviet missiles in Cuba were very modern and very dangerous. So the Soviets came to realize that their position would probably be hurt more by trying to link the missiles in Cuba with those in Turkey than by agreeing to withdraw their missiles from Cuba in exchange for a pledge by Kennedy not to invade.

16. In the aftermath of the crisis, President Kennedy agreed to a TV interview with Sandy Vanocur on Sunday evening, December 17, and he asked me to come chat with him that morning about the Soviet mood, bringing along with me one of the Bureau's Soviet specialists. I took Joseph Neubert, a career foreign service officer who had done a brilliant job of analysis during the crisis. When we arrived the president was seated in the sunroom alcove at the end of the Indian room in his private quarters, with the morning light pouring in and the Sunday papers scattered all around him. He was reading Khrushchev's long speech defending his decision to withdraw the missiles.

As we came in, the president looked up and said, "Listen to this." He then read us examples of the images Khrushchev had used in his speech—the one about the "smell of burning in the air" and also that the West might be a "paper tiger" but it still had "nuclear teeth." "Now those," he said, "are first-rate," and he proceeded to telephone Arthur Schlesinger to twit him about how good his rival speechwriters in the Kremlin were.

Chapter 8

The Aftermath

Even though Kennedy was elated when he talked to his brother, he avoided showing his feelings in public, and he cautioned the members of his administration against any tendency to gloat or claim a victory. For what President Kennedy really wanted was to use the crisis as a stepping-stone to a lessening of tensions in the world and a detente with the Soviet Union. Quite clearly, he was already thinking of what became his great American University speech that proposed a nuclear test ban treaty—which he hoped would be only the first step toward worldwide nuclear disarmament.

But such prospects were still in the future. In the immediate aftermath of the crisis, there were long and delicate exchanges about what the agreement really meant.

One issue was UN inspection. This had been part of the agreement, but the Soviets had neglected to get Castro's approval of the arrangement, and he flatly refused to permit it. As Castro had said earlier, "Whoever tries to inspect Cuba must come in battle array."

But the Soviets were accommodating. When American aircraft buzzed the outgoing Soviet freighters, the crews of the ships—undoubtedly under orders from Moscow—obligingly drew back the canvas tarpaulins covering the missiles so the American planes could take pictures.

Another issue was whether the IL–28 light bombers were included in the weapons to be returned to the Soviet Union. The range and payload of these planes were too small to be a real threat to the United States, but for domestic political reasons it was important that *no* weapons that could be termed "offensive" remained. The Soviets came to understand this and agreed to remove the IL–28s along with the missiles. The IL–28s, however, had already been turned over to Cuban control, and Castro balked. It was not until November 19 that Soviet pressure on Castro prevailed. Khrushchev announced that the IL–28s would be returned to the Soviet Union, and Kennedy announced that the quarantine would be lifted.

But in announcing Khrushchev's agreement to remove the IL–28s and permit their departure to be observed from the air on November 20, President Kennedy made it clear that in view of the refusal of the Cuban government to permit inspection or the setting up of lasting safeguards against the future introduction of offensive weapons into Cuba, the United States would continue its air reconnaissance activities.

Because of Castro's intransigence, the question of an American pledge not to invade Cuba also became an issue. Khrushchev wanted a written guarantee that the United States would not invade Cuba that would be binding not only on Kennedy himself but on future presidents as well. On December 10, Khrushchev wrote to Kennedy that he was "relying on your assurance that the United States and its allies will not invade Cuba." But in his reply on December 14, Kennedy made it clear that what the United States did in the future depended upon what Castro did in the future:

> We have never wanted to be driven by the acts of others into war in Cuba. The other side of the coin, however, is that we do need to have adequate assurances that all offensive weapons are removed from Cuba and are not reintroduced, and that Cuba itself commits no aggressive acts against any of the nations of the Western Hemisphere.

Another issue concerned Soviet troops and military technicians. Although this was not a specific part of the agreement, the United

States certainly desired that the Soviets troops, too, be withdrawn. Khrushchev's response here was also politically sensitive. But resolution of this issue required that the United States be sensitive to Khrushchev's political problem as well, which the Sino-Soviet dispute undoubtedly aggravated, and that the United States be patient about just how soon the Soviet troops would go. The troops associated with the missiles departed with the missiles. The rest, Khrushchev said, were in Cuba only to train the Cubans to operate the antiaircraft SAMs and other defensive equipment, and they would depart progressively as the training job was completed.

HAWKS IN THE CONGRESS

In the meantime, in the United States the militantly uncompromising anti-Communists kept up a steady barrage of charges that the Soviets were cheating on the agreements. Many of these charges were inspired by the Cuban refugees, whose only hope of returning to Cuba was on the back of a U.S. invasion. A particularly persistent charge inspired by the refugees was that the missiles were not really being taken out of Cuba, in spite of the photographs, but were being stored in caves. Some of the wilder charges were that complete installations had been built underground—including "airfields, missile platforms, and rocket storage facilities." But no one could explain how an airfield could be built underground.[1]

Senators Barry Goldwater and Kenneth Keating were particularly active. Goldwater said that he was not convinced that the Soviets had removed their missiles and that he knew "some darned good military men who don't think so either." He said that he thought the president would have "to face up to the necessity of an invasion."

On January 1, 1963, Senator Keating not only suggested that the Soviets had hidden the missiles in caves, but charged that new shipments of military equipment were arriving steadily and that the Soviets had not dismantled the missile sites but were maintaining and guarding them. Keating continued to make these charges even after the Defense Department released low-level reconnaissance photographs showing that the concrete revetments had been broken up by air hammers.

But much more seriously, the speeches of Senator Keating and

Senator Goldwater came very near to wrecking the agreement on troop withdrawal. Their charges and continual public harangues so exacerbated the Soviet leaders' own political situation that they raised the question of reversing their decision on removing the troops. Eventually, they went through with it, but it is clear that Goldwater's and Keating's intervention delayed the withdrawal of Soviet troops for a considerable period of time.

TYING UP SOME LOOSE ENDS

In 1987 during a conference on the crisis including American scholars and three Soviet officials, the Soviet representatives said that the decision to shoot down Major Anderson's U–2 was made by the local commander without authorization from Moscow. The fact that the Soviets would admit their lack of control over a local commander makes their account very credible.

Some of the other points that the Soviet representatives made also seem credible and are also new and different from what the Americans at the time understood.

At the time of the crisis, Washington was uncertain whether the request for missiles had come from Castro or Castro had requested arms and perhaps Soviet troops and the Soviets had seized on the request as an opportunity for a temporary solution to the "missile gap in reverse," telling Castro that they would supply the weapons he wanted if he would in turn give the Soviet Union permission to deploy nuclear missiles in Cuba. The Soviet representatives at the conference said that it was Khrushchev and the Soviets who initiated the proposal, and the Cuban representatives confirmed that statement.

A second point was that whereas U.S. intelligence had estimated the total Soviet military personnel at about 20,000, the Soviet representatives said that the actual figure was 42,000. What made this statement persuasive was the fact that in 1979 American intelligence discovered that a Soviet brigade of 2,600 men had stayed on in Cuba after the crisis.

However, another assertion by the Soviet representatives is not credible—that the approach by Fomin, the head of the KGB in Washington, was his own idea. As described above, Fomin asked

Scali if he would ask me to get a message to the president himself. Scali said that he thought I would do it if I was convinced that the message did indeed come from Khrushchev. Fomin stressed from the beginning that the message came directly from Khrushchev and that he, Fomin, was acting on Khrushchev's personal instructions. And Fomin repeated these statements several times. Without those emphatic assurances, I would not have taken the message to the secretary of state and the president. What was also convincing at the time, as mentioned above, was that the Soviets had used similar unofficial channels on many occasions in the past.

As mentioned in an endnote in the preceding chapter, it transpired years later that another KGB agent had approached U Thant with a strikingly similar proposal. So the Soviet practice, described by the analysts in INR, of using deniable channels to convey a message was in fact repeated in the Cuban missile crisis. What is more, U Thant was given to understand that Gromyko knew all about the approach, apparently to make him pay particular attention.

So the assertion that Fomin had acted on his own is hardly credible if another KGB agent was simultaneously approaching U Thant with what was almost exactly the same message.

As for the denials, the Soviets had an obvious interest in insisting that they were *not* using Fomin in an official approach. They had a large stake in keeping the approach unofficial and "deniable" at the time. If the United States refused the deal, they could simply say that Fomin had not been authorized to make it. At the time of this conference, the Soviet leaders still had a continuing interest in holding to that position in case such a channel might be useful again in the future.

In addition, I have been told by a Soviet official who was a personal aide to Foreign Minister Andrei Gromyko that the approach had indeed been instituted by Khrushchev.

Finally, it is simply not conceivable that if Fomin had been acting on his own he would have gone so far as to fabricate the very pointed message after the crisis was over conveying Khrushchev's thanks to Scali for his help. If Fomin had been acting on his own, he certainly would have had no incentive to take the additional risk of pretending to convey Khrushchev's thanks, since it was certainly obvious to Fomin that Scali's role would sooner or later be acknowledged in public. Indeed, when we asked Scali not to make his role public in the immediate aftermath of the crisis, we promised that in due time one or another high official would give him our public thanks.

Another conference between Americans and Soviets, which included people who had held higher-ranking positions during the crisis, was held in Moscow in 1988, as mentioned earlier. At this meeting, the Soviet representatives continued to peddle the line that the motive for the deployment of missiles to Cuba was fear that the United States was about to launch an invasion to make up for the failure of the Bay of Pigs. However, since the Soviets knew that Kennedy had adamantly refused to give in to the pressure to use American air and naval forces at the time of the Bay of Pigs, it is hardly credible that fear of an American invasion was the reason for the deployment in 1962.

Also, an invasion fleet takes an enormous number of landing craft. The United States had not assembled those landing craft at the time the Soviet decision was made to send the missiles to Cuba, and Soviet intelligence had excellent means to make that determination. It is simply inconceivable that they failed to use those means before making such a fateful decision if the decision to deploy the missiles had really been based on fear of an American invasion.

NOTE

1. *New York Times,* November 28, 1962.

Chapter 9

The Significance

No one would argue that the Cuban missile crisis did not pose extreme dangers. But just how great were the risks of actual war?

It is crystal clear that both Kennedy and Khrushchev very quickly decided not only that nuclear war was unthinkable but also that it was unthinkable to run any risk at all of such a war if it could be avoided, even a very small risk. Neither was seeking a confrontation, and both were doing everything they could to avoid one.

Kennedy and many other members of the ExCom clearly saw the blockade as only the first step in a long series of moves short of war. The arrangement that Kennedy made with Andrew Cordier for U Thant to request both sides to withdraw all their missiles stationed outside their borders when Kennedy gave the signal is one example of steps that he was planning down the road. Even if that particular ploy had not worked, Kennedy was a long way from actual fighting.

If an agreement to remove the missiles had not been reached when it was, within a few days Kennedy probably would have ordered the Air Force to destroy the SAM site that shot down Major Anderson's U–2. But the evidence is that his next step beyond that would have been to add oil, machinery, and other goods to the "quarantine" list until only food and medicine were left.

The Soviets were also cautious. Although it must be assumed that Khrushchev in prudence ordered an alert for the Soviet ICBM forces, he also seems to have taken care not to permit a general military alert.

Another piece of evidence concerns Berlin. During the early deliberations of the ExCom one of the greatest fears was that any U.S. action concerning Cuba would be countered by a Soviet move against Berlin. Yet it became clear as the crisis progressed that Khrushchev was studiously avoiding any move that could be interpreted as a threat to Berlin. That this decision was deliberate was confirmed in later years.

But in spite of the determination on both sides to avoid a nuclear war and in spite of all the precautions taken on both sides, it proved impossible to avoid dangerous misunderstandings, slips, missteps, and unauthorized actions by subordinates. The number of these potential disasters is frightening.

The greatest miscalculation, of course, was Khrushchev's original decision to send missiles to Cuba.

On the other hand, the United States also made an early miscalculation that was extremely serious. As already discussed, the Americans realized that the Soviets would be alarmed by the news in Gilpatric's speech and the NATO briefings that the United States had learned that the missile gap was in its favor. Yet American intelligence failed to see that one possible Soviet response would be to send missiles to Cuba. The result, as we saw, was that President Kennedy's various speeches and messages warning against putting offensive weapons in Cuba came not in the winter and early spring of 1962, when they might have influenced the Soviet decision to send missiles to Cuba, but in September—long after the decision had been made and its implementation begun.

The United States also came very near making a tragic miscalculation when it came so close to deciding to shoot down the Aeroflot plane thought to be carrying the nuclear warheads, rather than waiting until it landed to make certain of its cargo.

Another Soviet miscalculation was shooting down Major Anderson's U–2. In the 1987 conference to discuss the crisis, already described, held in Cambridge, Massachusetts, the Soviet representatives asserted that the decision to shoot down the U–2 was made without consulting Moscow by a Soviet one-star general, Igor D. Statsenko.[1] However, General Issa Pliyev was in overall command of the Soviet forces in Cuba, while Statsenko was in command only of the missile forces, and it seemed unlikely that chain of command over the SAMs would run through the missile force commander.

Then at another conference in 1989 in Moscow, the Soviet participants said that the decision to shoot down the U–2 was made by two other Soviet generals, Pliyev's deputy for air defense, General Stepan N. Grechko, and his deputy for military training, General Leonid S. Garbuz. In any case, the point is that the decision to shoot down the U–2 was made by Soviet officers in Cuba without consulting Moscow.

The ExCom had decided, to repeat, that if a U–2 was shot down, the SAM installation responsible would be immediately destroyed. If a second U–2 was attacked, then *all* the SAMs would be taken out. However, when the shoot-down actually occurred, President Kennedy decided to hold off the retaliation until the American response to the package of Khrushchev's cable and the approach through Fomin could be sent and a reply received. If he had not held back, the Soviets might have decided that they, too, must retaliate against the retaliation. Thus the situation could have quickly spiraled into war—a frightening thought.

But it is even more frightening that the Kremlin had such little control over the troops in the field that a local commander could order the U–2 to be shot down without authority from Moscow. The fact that the Soviets admitted that they had so little control makes it entirely credible.

The violation of Soviet airspace by the American U–2 on an air-sampling mission to the North Pole in the midst of the crisis was equally frightening. As Khrushchev said, it could easily have been misinterpreted as a reconnaissance in advance of a preemptive nuclear attack. Humankind is fortunate that Khrushchev, like Kennedy, held back.

Another major slip was the harsh Moscow Radio broadcast on Saturday morning that seemed to reverse the proposals contained in Khrushchev's cable and the Fomin approach the night before. If the analysts in INR had failed to notice the language differences that indicated that the Moscow broadcast predated the Khrushchev-Fomin approach and if Robert Kennedy had not come up with the Trollope ploy, the crisis might have escalated very rapidly.

Another dangerous American miscalculation was discovered only later, and it illustrates why civilian authorities are sometimes nervous about the military. It turned out that General Thomas S. Power had on his own authority decided to send the message alerting SAC in the clear. He did so knowing that the Soviets would intercept the message, and he did so deliberately, on the grounds that the Soviets would be intimidated by the message. Sending such a message in the clear in the expectation that the Soviets would intercept it and that it would affect their behavior was not only unauthorized but provocative. It was a clear act of insubordination.

Another act of insubordination occurred when the Navy disobeyed Kennedy's order to put the blockade line close to the Cuban shore so Khrushchev would have time to consider the Soviet response, rather than well out to sea in accordance with tradition. Although the Navy's action did not increase the danger, it was not only insubordinate but grossly insensitive to the political implications as well.

A Soviet act of provocation was testing the blockade by sending one of the halted ships speeding toward Cuba—especially since it was obviously fully authorized by Moscow. The fact that the United States took care to determine what kind of ship it was and discovered that it was a tanker and could not carry missiles does not alter the fact that the act was provocative. What if Kennedy had not decided to let it go unchallenged? The Soviet submarines escorting it would probably have attacked the challenging American vessel, and what would have happened then?

A truly dangerous action on the part of the American Navy was forcing Soviet submarines to surface to recharge their batteries in the presence of American warships. Kennedy had not forbidden such action, not only because he didn't know about them but also because it would have been inconceivable to him that in such tense circumstances anyone would even contemplate such risky actions. Even more alarming was the fact, as we learned only much later, that the Navy had even used practice depth charges on some occasions to force some of the Soviet submarines to the surface.

The lesson is overwhelmingly obvious. No matter how cautious the leaders on both sides may be, in an international crisis, dangerous misunderstandings, slips, missteps, and unauthorized actions by subordinates simply cannot be avoided. But when the consequences can be nuclear war any risk at all is simply unacceptable. For at least some of the people who participated in the crisis decisions, this came to be the dominating and most urgent lesson to be learned. It led them, as described below, to a fundamental change in their attitude toward the whole concept of deterrence.

WHY DID THE SOVIETS BACK DOWN?

The risks to both sides in the Cuban missile crisis were real, direct, and very high. As Dean Rusk said, a misstep might have meant the "incineration" of the entire Northern Hemisphere, east and west. Even so, it is not possible to say that it was the nuclear threat, as such, that caused the Soviets to back down. The Soviet leaders probably had considerable confidence in the judgment, restraint, and sense of responsibility of the American leaders, and they undoubtedly assumed the American response would begin with conventional means and would continue to be restricted to conventional means unless the Soviets themselves did something that raised the ante to the nuclear level.

On the other hand, it is also not possible to say that the Soviets backed down solely in the face of a threat to invade Cuba with conventional, nonnuclear forces, even though they knew that the troops they had in Cuba could not stand up to such an invasion. The Soviet leadership often repeated, and only in part for self-serving motives, that limited war would always carry a risk of escalation to nuclear war. And certainly in the Cuban missile crisis there were a number of ways that events could have gotten out of hand and escalated into a nuclear conflagration.

If the crisis had not been resolved when it was, for example, events could have escalated until the United States launched an invasion. The Soviet troops were armed with battlefield nuclear weapons, as described in Chapter 7, and the commander had advance permission to use them against an invading force. The preliminary American plans provided tactical nuclear weapons for the invasion force, and even if the president had decided that they should not actually accompany the troops, they could have been brought forward very quickly. In such circumstances, the crisis could easily have spiraled out of control.

But Khrushchev and the top Soviet leadership were as sensitive to the risks as Kennedy and the ExCom were—and also just as sensitive to the need for a quick resolution before one side or the other lost control.

Some observers have tried to find still undiscovered reasons why Khrushchev backed down in what seemed to be a sudden decision.[2] It is known, for example, that Castro sent Khrushchev a still-secret cable. The cable is reported to have said that Castro had intelligence that an American invasion was imminent and demanded that the Soviets preempt the invasion with a nuclear strike on the United States; and the speculation is that this pushed Khrushchev into a precipitate decision.[3]

There has also been speculation that Castro was planning to seize control of the missiles and fire them. But there has been no shred of evidence to support this speculation, and the fact is the Soviet ground forces in Cuba could have defeated the whole Cuban army in very short order.

But it seems not only credible but obvious that the sense of urgency that Khrushchev felt was the same that Kennedy felt—that the longer the crisis went on the greater were the chances of misunderstandings, slips, missteps, and unauthorized actions by subordinates and the greater were the chances that one or the other of these might be fatal.

On balance, in other words, the best judgment seems to be that the Soviets backed down in the face of a threat that combined both conventional and nuclear power. Cuba was close to the sources of American strength and distant from the sources of Soviet strength. With vastly shorter lines of communication, the United States could apply overwhelming conventional power at the point of contact— Cuba. But the United States could apply that conventional power under an umbrella of nuclear power that foreclosed any possibility of the Soviets trying to use nuclear weapons to redress the imbalance at the contact point. It was this combination of overwhelming conventional power on the spot and fully adequate nuclear power overall that proved irresistible.

Let it also be said that the decision to withdraw the missiles required courage on the Soviet side and that although putting the missiles in Cuba was threatening and irresponsible, the Soviets handled the ensuing crisis with wisdom and restraint. Khrushchev personally deserves much of the credit, but other Soviet leaders share in it.

As it worked out, none of the IRBMs actually arrived in Cuba, but *all* of the MRBMs were operational by October 28. My own feeling is that the United States would and should have gone on to invade if the Soviets had not agreed to withdraw their missiles, but even so it is awesome to contemplate the situation of American ground and air forces attacking Soviet nuclear missiles poised on their pads and defended by Soviet ground combat forces equipped with tactical nuclear weapons.

In any case, the first and most obvious answer to the question of why the Soviets backed down is that of power and will. The United States decided to accept the Soviet challenge, and American strength and determination were sufficient to meet the challenge. The United States had both the power and the will, and the Soviet Union suffered a defeat.

But it would be a mistake to conclude that this same formula of will and power can be translated into success in every kind of confrontation—that it would necessarily have worked in Laos, for example, or Vietnam. The arena in the Cuba case was close to the sources of American power, to repeat, and far from the sources of Soviet power. But, more importantly, there was no doubt at all about the stakes: the threat from Cuba in October, 1962, was nuclear, and it was directed at the American heartland.

It would also be a mistake to think that the formula of will and power is appropriate to all political objectives. The issue here is the relationship of means to ends—the appropriateness and acceptability both to world opinion and to the conscience of the American people of using military force to accomplish particular objectives. It is acceptable and fitting that the United States use the full panoply of its military power to remove a threat to its survival. But at some point as one moves down the scale from national survival to progressively lesser objectives, the political cost of using raw military force begins to exceed the potential gain. When that point is reached the wise nation shifts away from military force as the means to achieve its goals and adopts other instrumentalities.

Reasonable people may quarrel about the wisdom of the exact point at which President Kennedy chose to make this shift in the Cuban missile crisis. He chose to shift just after the removal of the missiles but before the withdrawal of Soviet advisers and the elimination of the Castro regime. Reasonable people might argue for making the shift at some different point, but they would not question the principle itself.

THE HISTORICAL SIGNIFICANCE

Because we still live in a nuclear world, we cannot see the final meaning of the Cuban missile crisis or measure the full dimensions of its place in the history of humankind. But surely any assessment of its significance must begin with the fact that it was the first nuclear crisis the world has ever seen and that what President Kennedy and the United States did in meeting the crisis set precedents applicable to all the subsequent international crises of our time.

The keynote of the U.S. response was flexibility and self-disciplined restraint—a graduated effort that avoided trying to achieve too much and that stopped short of confronting its adversary with stark and imperative choices. Out of that basic policy flowed the precedents—restraint in the use of power; flexibility in developing a solution; the pacing of events to give the other side time to think and so obviate "spasm reactions"; the "making of a little international law" outlawing the secret and rapid deployment of nuclear weapons, as Abram Chayes said; the deliberate regard for precedent and the effect of present actions on the longer-range future; and, finally, the relevancy of moral integrity to that longer-range future—a point on which both the president and his brother Robert so strongly insisted.

Whether the Cuban missile crisis marked a turning point in world history is as yet impossible to say. The Soviets put missiles in Cuba in an attempt to solve a particular set of problems—a strategic imbalance, the exigencies of the Sino-Soviet dispute, and the impossible combination of demands on their limited resources made by defense, their space program, their people's appetite for consumer goods, and the drain of foreign aid needed to support their foreign policy. When the crisis was over and the missiles withdrawn, the same set of problems remained.

One irony is that these same problems, which brought the world so near to nuclear war, later brought about the so-called detente—a relaxation of Cold War tensions. For it was the same pressures that led the Soviets to put missiles in Cuba that later led them to take up Kennedy's proposal in his American University speech for a treaty banning nuclear testing.

The nuclear test ban treaty that Kennedy had in mind included on-site inspections. The Soviets had flatly rejected inspection on all the previous occasions on which it had been raised. The reason was simple. A police state simply cannot tolerate international inspectors wandering around. The only way that a police state can remain a police state is to keep its people ignorant of the outside world. This time, however, Khrushchev was willing to permit three UN inspections a year. The Pentagon insisted that there be a minimum of five, and nothing the president said or did could shake their determination. He met just as solid a stone wall when he tried to get the Soviets to agree to five.

Kennedy felt certain that if he agreed to three inspections rather than five, the hard-liners in the Pentagon lobbying the hard-liners in Congress would defeat the treaty. But Kennedy felt that half a loaf at that point would permit him to come back in a year or two and get the other half, so he agreed to a treaty with no inspections at all as a first step. He did not calculate on being assassinated.

Following the crisis, the Soviets had only two alternatives. One was a crash ICBM program to redress the strategic imbalance. This would require austerity at home, and a return to the coldest kind of Cold War abroad. The Communist world would have to close ranks, and so, as a most unpalatable corollary, the Sino-Soviet dispute would have to be healed, even if the Chinese demanded that it be on their terms.

The other alternative was the one the Soviets actually chose— easing the tensions of the Cold War, with the limited test ban treaty as the first concrete step. The Soviet ICBM program could then be stretched out, and the burdens lightened of competing so aggressively in the underdeveloped world. And this course of action also had a corollary for the Sino-Soviet dispute—a sharpening of the tension between Communist China and the Soviet Union.

But the Cuban missile crisis quite clearly had deeper, more profound, and longer-range effects.

One of the longer-range effects was to change attitudes toward nuclear weapons. Before the Cuban missile crisis, most of the American officials who later participated in the crisis deliberations accepted Churchill's notion of a balance of terror. They assumed that to keep the peace all that the United States needed to do was to make certain that its nuclear forces were adequate, to maintain the will and determination to use those weapons if the worst came to the worst, and to take appropriate steps to ensure that the other side understood all this. Presumably, the Soviet leaders had reached a similar set of conclusions.

For many of the people involved in the crisis the lesson, as we said, was that the risk of an inadvertent escalation during a crisis was unavoidable and that in a nuclear age such risk was unacceptable. The leaders of both the Soviet Union and the United States had gazed down the gun barrel of nuclear war and had shrunk back from the holocaust they saw there.

But many of the participants on both sides were shocked and deeply troubled by the many missteps and unauthorized actions. Their faith in both deterrence and Churchill's balance of terror was deeply shaken.

The more one looked at the awesome consequences of nuclear war, the clearer it became that the old verities of international politics must be reexamined. Germany, for example, seemed less a threat in a nuclear age. In fact, the entire political landscape of Eastern Europe looked different. Thinking about the implications of the Cuban missile crisis contributed substantially to the series of events that led finally to the breakup of the Soviet Union.

The threat of a nuclear holocaust will clearly make all nations more careful, and this caution might well preserve the peace for years and even decades. But after the Cuban missile crisis it seemed painfully clear that if nuclear weapons were allowed to remain in the world's arsenals sooner or later another nuclear crisis would occur. One, two, or even three more nuclear crises might be handled with equal success. But sooner or later a crisis would occur in which the leaders on both sides were not so prudent as Kennedy and Khrushchev had been. In one crisis or another even greater slips and miscalculations would be inevitable. The conclusion seemed inescapable to many of the participants that if nuclear weapons and the missiles to deliver them are allowed to remain in the world's arsenals, sooner or later there will be a nuclear holocaust.

But that conclusion is only a first step. Both Great Britain and the United States began serious efforts to build an atomic bomb only after World War II had already begun. But they succeeded. Suppose the nations of the world agreed to abolish nuclear weapons. But suppose that a series of events brought the major powers into a new world war. The pressures on all the warring powers to build nuclear weapons would be enormous—people on both sides would echo

President Truman's words about the H-bomb, "If the enemy can build this thing, how can we not build it?" And they would be able to build the bombs and the missiles to deliver them much more quickly for the simple reason that they already would know how.

The conclusion is as obvious as it is insistent. Abolishing nuclear weapons will not be enough. If humankind is to avoid Armageddon, it must abolish war itself.

NOTES

1. Raymond L. Garthoff, "Cuban Missile Crisis: The Soviet Story," *Foreign Policy* (Fall, 1988). The Soviet ambassador to Cuba, Aleksandr Alekseyev, said that the order was the result of a "trigger-happy Soviet air defense commander." However, Sergo Mikoyan said that General Statsenko did command the Soviet forces in Cuba, in spite of his relatively low rank. Mikoyan also said that just before his death in October, 1987, Statsenko confided that he was the one who made the decision to fire.

2. One indication of the suddenness, it has been argued, is that he so quickly dropped his demand for the removal of the American missiles in Turkey.

3. Bruce J. Allyn, James G. Blight, and David A. Welch, "Essence of Revision: Moscow, Havana, and the Cuban Missile Crisis," *International Security*, Vol. 14, No. 3 (Winter, 1989/90).

Bibliography

BOOKS

Abel, Elie. *The Cuban Missile Crisis*. New York: Praeger, 1966.

Allison, Graham T. *Essence of Decision: Explaining the Cuban Missile Crisis*. Boston: Little, Brown, 1971.

Beschloss, Michael R. *The Crisis Years: Kennedy and Khrushchev*. New York: Edward Burlingame Books, 1991.

Blight, James G. *On the Brink: Americans and Soviets Reexamine the Cuban Missile Crisis*. New York: Hill and Wang, 1989.

———. *The Shattered Crystal Ball: Fear and Learning in the Cuban Missile Crisis*. Savage, MD: Rowman & Littlefield, 1990.

Blight, James G.; Allyn, Bruce J.; and Welch, David A. *Cuba on the Brink: Castro, the Missile Crisis, and the Soviet Collapse*. New York: Pantheon Books, 1993.

Bowles, Chester. *Promises to Keep*. New York: Harper and Row, 1965.

Brugioni, Dino A. *Eyeball to Eyeball: The Inside Story of the Cuban Missile Crisis*. New York: Random House, 1991.

Brune, Lester H. *The Missile Crisis of October 1962: A Review of Issues and References*. Claremont, CA: Regina Books, 1985.

Bundy, McGeorge. *Danger and Survival: Choices about the Bomb in the First Fifty Years*. New York: Random House, 1988.

Caldwell, Dan. *Soviet-American Crisis Management in the Cuban Missile Crisis and the October War*. Santa Monica, CA: California Seminar on International Security and Foreign Policy, 1981.

Chang, Laurence and Kornbluh, Peter. *The Cuban Missile Crisis, 1962: A National Security Archive Reader*. New York: The New Press, 1992.

Chayes, Abram. *The Cuban Missile Crisis: International Crisis and the Role of Law*. New York: Oxford University Press, 1974.

Detzer, David. *The Brink: Cuban Missile Crisis*. New York: Crowell, 1979.

Dinerstein, Herbert S. *The Making of a Missile Crisis, October 1962*. Baltimore: Johns Hopkins Press, 1976.

Garthoff, Raymond L. *Intelligence Assessment and Policymaking: A Decision Point in the Kennedy Administration*. Washington, DC: The Brookings Institution, 1984.

Garthoff, Raymond L. *Reflections on the Cuban Missile Crisis*. Washington, DC: The Brookings Institution, 1987.

Gribkov, A. I. *Operation ANADYR: U.S. and Soviet Generals Recount the Cuban Missile Crisis*. Chicago: Edition Q., 1994.

Hilsman, Roger. *To Move a Nation: The Politics of Foreign Policy in the Administration of John F. Kennedy*. Garden City, NY: Doubleday, 1967.

Hilsman, Roger, with Laura Gaughran and Patricia Weitsman. *The Politics of Policy Making in Defense and Foreign Affairs: Conceptual Models and Bureaucratic Politics*. 3rd ed. Englewood Cliffs, NJ: Prentice Hall, 1993.

Kennedy, Robert F. *Thirteen Days: A Memoir of the Cuban Missile Crisis*. New York: W. W. Norton, 1969.

Khrushchev, Nikita. *Khrushchev Remembers: The Last Testament*. Trans. and ed. by Strobe Talbot. Boston: Little, Brown, 1974.

Leighton, Richard M. *The Cuban Missile Crisis of 1962: A Case in National Security Crisis Management*. Washington, DC: Department of Defense, National Defense University, 1978.

McAuliffe, Mary S., ed. *CIA Documents on the Cuban Missile Crisis, 1962*. Washington, DC: History Staff, Central Intelligence Agency, October, 1992.

Medland, William J. *The Cuban Missile Crisis of 1962: Needless or Necessary?* New York: Praeger, 1988.

O'Brian, Lawrence F. *No Final Victories.* Garden City, NY: Doubleday, 1974.

Pope, Ronald R. *Soviet Views on the Cuban Missile Crisis: Myth and Reality in Foreign Policy Analysis.* Lanham, MD: University Press of America, 1982.

————. *The "Cuban Crisis" of 1962: Selected Documents, Chronology, and Bibliography.* Lanham, MD: University Press of America, 1986.

Power, General Thomas S., with Albert A. Arnhym. *Design for Survival.* New York: Coward-McCann, 1965.

Schlesinger, Arthur M., Jr. *A Thousand Days: John F. Kennedy in the White House.* Boston: Houghton-Mifflin, 1965.

Sorensen, Theodore C. *Kennedy.* New York: Harper and Row, 1965.

Thompson, Robert Smith. *The Missiles of October: The Declassified Story of John F. Kennedy and the Cuban Missile Crisis.* New York: Simon and Schuster, 1992.

Young, John M. *When the Russians Blinked: The U.S. Maritime Response to the Cuban Missile Crisis.* Occasional paper series, U.S. Marine Corps, History and Museums Division, Headquarters, U.S. Marine Corps, 1990.

ARTICLES

Allyn, Bruce J.; Blight, James G.; and Welch, David A. "Essence of Revision: Moscow, Havana, and the Cuban Missile Crisis." *International Security,* Vol. 14, No. 3 (Winter, 1989/90).

Art, Robert J. "Bureaucratic Politics and American Foreign Policy: A Critique." *Policy Sciences* (December, 1974).

Bernstein, Barton J. "The Cuban Missile Crisis: Trading the Jupiters in Turkey?" *Political Science Quarterly* (Spring, 1980).

Blight, James G.; Nye, Joseph S.; and Welch, David A. "The Cuban Missile Crisis Revisited." *Foreign Affairs* (Fall, 1987).

Cline, Ray S. "The Cuban Missile Crisis: Commentary." *Foreign Affairs,* Vol. 68 (Fall, 1989).

Garthoff, Raymond L. "Cuban Missile Crisis: The Soviet Story." *Foreign Policy* (Fall, 1988).

Hafner, Donald L. "Bureaucratic Politics and 'Those Frigging Missiles': JFK, Cuba and U.S. Missiles in Turkey." *Orbis* (Summer, 1977).

Hughes, Thomas L. *The Fate of Facts in a World of Men: Foreign Policy and Intelligence-Making.* New York: The Foreign Policy Association, Headline Series No. 233, 1976, p. 44.

Lebow, Richard Ned. "The Cuban Missile Crisis: Reading the Lessons Correctly." *Political Science Quarterly* (Fall, 1983).

Pohlmann, Marcus D. "Constraining Presidents at the Brink: The Cuban Missile Crisis." *Presidential Studies Quarterly,* Vol. 19 (Spring, 1989).

Problems of Communism. Vol. 41 (Spring, 1992). The entire issue is devoted to the Cuban missile crisis.

Scott, Len and Smith, Steve. "Lessons of October: Historians, Political Scientist, Policy-makers and the Cuban Missile Crisis." *International Affairs* (October, 1994).

Welch, David A. and Blight, James G. "The Eleventh Hour of the Cuban Missile Crisis: An Introduction to the ExCom Transcripts." *International Security* (Winter, 1987/1988).

————. "October 27, 1962: Transcripts of the Meetings of the ExComm." *International Security* (Winter, 1987/1988).

Wohlstetter, Roberta. "Cuba and Pearl Harbor: Hindsight and Foresight." *Foreign Affairs* (July, 1965).

Index

About the Author

ROGER HILSMAN graduated from West Point in 1943, was severely wounded serving with Merrill's Marauders in Burma, and later commanded a battalion of guerrillas operating behind the enemy lines. He earned masters and doctoral degrees in world politics at Yale, taught at Princeton, and then served as deputy director of the Congressional Research Service. In 1961, President Kennedy appointed him Assistant Secretary of State for Intelligence and Research and later Assistant Secretary for Far Eastern Affairs. In 1964, he resigned to accept a professorship at Columbia University. He has authored or coauthored 14 books examining American foreign policy and diplomatic and military affairs. His wartime memoir, *American Guerrilla: My War Behind Japanese Lines* was published in 1990.